ANCIENT SITES
OF MAUI,
MOLOKA'I,
AND LĀNA'I

REVISED & EXPANDED EDITION

A Guide to
**Hawaiian Archaeological
and Cultural Places of Interest**

VAN JAMES

Mutual
Publishing

To the memory of
Evan E. James
I ulu nō ka lālā i ke kumu.
The branches grow from the trunk.
[We are here because of our ancestors.]

And to the dreams of
Veronica James Yard,
Terrence Kahekili, Tyson Laʻakea, and Kalila Lehua Ozaki
ʻUkuliʻi ka pua, onaona i ka mauʻu.
Tiny is the flower, yet it scents the grasses all around.
[Said of a young person who gives joy to others.]

OTHER BOOKS BY THE AUTHOR:

Ancient Sites of Oʻahu
*Archaeological Places of Interest
in the Hawaiian Islands*

Ancient Sites of Hawaiʻi
*Archaeological Places of Interest
on the Big Island*

Ancient Sites of Kauaʻi
*A Guide to Hawaiian
Archaeological and Cultural Places*

Spirit and Art
*Pictures of the Transformation
of Consciousness*

The Secret Language of Form
Visual Meaning in Art and Nature

**Drawing with Hand,
Head and Heart**
*A Natural Approach
to Learning the Art of Drawing*

Copyright © 2001 by Van James
New edition © 2018 by Van James
Published by Mutual Publishing

All photographs and illustrations
by Van James unless otherwise indicated.

First printing (new edition), May 2018

Mutual Publishing, LLC
1215 Center Street, Suite 210
Honolulu, Hawaiʻi 96816
Ph: (808) 732-1709
Fax: (808) 734-4094
Email: info@mutualpublishing.com
www.mutualpublishing.com

Library of Congress Control Number:
  2017933300
ISBN-13: 978-1939487-73-5

Printed in China

CONTENTS

Satellite photo of Moloka'i, Lāna'i, Maui and Kaho'olawe. (Wikimedia Commons)

FOREWORD

When I received a call from Van James asking if I would consider writing the Foreword for this publication, two thoughts immediately came to mind. The first was the modern Hawaiian way of hospitality and giving freely of personal wealth, and the second was keeping our cultural practices and sacred places secret.

Due to religious and political condemnation and exploitation of our practices and places, Hawaiians were conditioned to protect their sacred practices and sites. However, in recent years a change of attitude has emerged. This new attitude is based on the belief that education and awareness will bring understanding, respect, and compassion, and, therefore, this education and awareness could lead to the preservation of our culture, language, and ancient sites.

There are, however, those practices and places that are still so dear and sacred to us that it is not yet the proper time to share them. They represent a link so crucial to us that premature exposure may cause irreparable harm to our existence as kanaka maoli.

This brought about my second thought, which was exactly which sites were being considered in this publication and were they being properly represented. After all, there are thousands of ancient and sacred sites throughout Maui alone, much less the other islands.

The obvious solution was to ask for a copy of the transcripts and a copy of any previous publications. Without hesitation, Van James accommodated my request and, as they say, the rest is history.

The waiwai (true worth) of our culture is found in our language, practices, and in the evidence our ancestors left behind on the land. We commonly refer to them as ancient sites and sacred sites. In many cases this evidence is in the form of physical features and stories. However, in most cases the evidence is the mere beauty and natural surroundings they preserved for us. What they also left for us is the ability to see beauty, life, and love in everything.

Our ancestors received their wisdom from everything around them. They revered all the things that gave them nourishment whether it was in the form of food, wisdom, or spirituality. Van James is obviously well aware of this and it is reflected in this publication. *Ancient Sites of Maui, Moloka‘i and Lāna‘i* is well thought out, researched, and sensitive to the varying interpretations of the ancient stories. It highlights a richness of this unique place and people. Thanks to Van James for excluding sites that are kapu (forbidden).

All sites are wahi pana (sacred), and it is important that, while there, we conduct ourselves properly. Reverence, humility, and compassion for the place and each other are paramount. Leaving a ho'okupu (offering) is a necessary practice of the Hawaiians. Ho'okupu usually represents something that sprouts, like foliage, rather than something modern, like a store-bought trinket. However, the highest and most meaningful ho'okupu is mai loko mai (comes from within). This means, your personal commitment to being a maoli (true person).

This publication provides a unique opportunity for malihini and kama'āina to share in the waiwai of Hawai'i. Mahalo to you, Van James, for this gift.

—Kahu Kapiiohookalani Lyons Naone
Kīpahulu, Maui, Hawai'i

PREFACE

I n ancient times, the sacred places of Hawai'i, or wahi pana of Hawai'i, were treated with great reverence and deference. These places possess spiritual power, mana, but the designation wahi pana means much more than just a sacred geographical spot. In Hawaiian culture, the idea of "place" itself holds deep meaning.

As a Native Hawaiian, a place tells me who I am and who my extended family is. A place gives me my history, the history of my clan, and the history of my people. I am able to look at a place and tie in human events that affect me and my loved ones. A place gives me a feeling of stability and of belonging to my family, those living and dead. A place gives me a sense of well-being and of acceptance of all who have experienced that place.

The concept of wahi pana merges the importance of place with that of the spiritual. My culture accepts the spiritual as a dominant factor in life; this value links me to my past and to my future, and is physically located at my wahi pana.

Where once the entire Native Hawaiian society paid homage to numerous wahi pana, now we may give wahi pana hardly a cursory glance. Only when a Native Hawaiian gains spiritual wisdom is the ancestral and spiritual sense of place reactivated. Spiritual knowledge and the wahi pana are ancestrally related, thus spiritual strength connects to the ancestral guardians, or 'aumākua. My 'aumākua knew that the great gods created the land and generated life. The gods infused the earth with their spiritual force or mana. The gravity of this concept was keenly grasped by my ancestors: they knew that the earth's spiritual essence was focused through the wahi pana.

My ancestors honored the earth and life as divine gifts of the gods. Their fishing and farming enterprises always included a spiritual function and focus on a wahi pana. Their activities never encouraged land or sea resource overuse because to do so would dishonor the gods. "The earth must not be desecrated" is a Native Hawaiian value.

The gods and their disciples specified places that were sacred. The inventory of sacred places in Hawai'i includes the dwelling places of the gods, the dwelling places of venerable disciples, temples, and shrines, as well as selected observation points, cliffs, mounds, mountains, weather phenomena, forests, and volcanoes. As my ancestral religion functions through a hierarchy of gods, practices, and lore, the wahi pana, too are hierarchical. A wahi pana favored by a dominant god or a high-status disciple is inherently more remarkable than one favored by a lesser god or being. The great god Kū is associated with the luakini heiau, or temple, while the lesser manifestation of Kū known as Kūʻula is associated with a lower order of fishing shrine.

The gods defined many wahi pana, but so did individuals, events, and functions. The south point of Hawaiʻi island, Ka Lae, is a wahi pana of long-distance voyaging and offshore fishing. Ka Lae served as a navigational reference for oceanic travel between Hawaiʻi and southern Polynesia, and priests communed there to use its mana in planning.

Though wahi pana are normally associated with geographical areas, this is not always so. For instance, Paliuli, a divine place of much spiritual presence, cannot be found with a map or jungle guide. Paliuli is discoverable only if one's mind and soul are ready to receive this wahi pana in the uplands of Hilo. Conversely, the water hole Palehemo, in the district of Kaʻū, gained spiritual status through functional use over many generations.

My ancestors and I believe in a life that integrates the world of the seen and the world of the unseen as complementary parts of a whole. My ancestors and I believe that a theme of lōkahi, or balance, is necessary for a healthy, natural existence. Both worlds are part of that theme, as are male and female, and day and night. Dualism was evident philosophically and physically in the life of my ancestors. Wahi pana were a part of this dualism, thus some wahi pana favor females, some favor males, and some are useful to both sexes.

I use the wahi pana in my practice of pono, or righteousness, which results in an increase in my mana. Use of wahi pana is most efficacious when the practitioner is a Native Hawaiian. Wahi pana rituals are usually performed when no uninvited guests are present; therefore, night and early morning ceremonies are typical. The rituals involve prayers, offerings, and conversations with deities. The rituals are closed because the ignorant often offend and desecrate rather than honor. Yet I have at times seen even foreigners, who have only read about the goddess Pele, bring acceptable offerings, such as food and foliage. The difference, of course, lies in individual sensitivity, thoughtfulness, and humility. These are the qualities needed to fully benefit from any wahi pana.

The wahi pana of Maui, Molokaʻi and Lānaʻi are part of my culture and values. These places need our protection and deference—not only for their historical significance, but also for their human significance. We Native Hawaiians offer to others many of the unique features of our culture, but sharing is not a one-way street. Any resource that is mined and consumed will become depleted if there is no attempt at conservation or replenishment. Overuse by tourists and the general public will result in the physical depletion of our sacred places and, subsequently, in the spiritual desecration of our wahi pana.

This guidebook approaches wahi pana with appropriate sensitivity, thoughtfulness, and humility. Those who visit and pay these sites the respect and deference they deserve, whether they are Native Hawaiian or not, will benefit from the experience of communing with the ancestors, learning the functions, and absorbing the spiritual power of the wahi pana. Study, observe, and appreciate, for these sites are part of spiritual wisdom.

—Edward L. H. Kanahele
(1942-2000)

INTRODUCTION

During the Hawaiian renaissance beginning in the 1970s and continuing to this day, a great reawakening of Hawaiian culture and values arose in these islands, sparked by a rediscovery of the traditional wisdom in everyday practices such as the language arts and storytelling, hula, many kinds of practical crafts, health care, and other vocational activities. One such field of rediscovery was navigation and long-distance sailing, which in the 1960s was thought by many academics to be a primitive, accidental practice of the early Polynesians. With a re-learning of phenomenological, non-instrument observation, ancient navigational skills were brought back into practice, rejuvenated with modern insights to demonstrate the great wisdom in finding one's course and direction by means of the stars, the wave patterns, flights of birds, and colors of clouds. This rediscovery of navigational skills led to a Pacific-wide rebirth in oceanic wayfinding.

One of the reasons for this guidebook on ancient sites of Maui, Moloka'i and Lāna'i is to encourage not only visitors to Hawai'i, but residents and kama'āina (children of the land), to familiarize themselves with the ancient legacy of this unique place in the Pacific. For just as the navigation of the seas can awaken us to certain oceanic wayfinding skills, so can the rediscovery of wahi pana, the storied landscape of a place, instruct us toward a greater awareness of the sacred lay-of-the-land, with its hills and valleys, gulches and ridges, the flow of its rock formations and vegetation, the quality of its land-shapes. What the Chinese call *feng shui* ("wind water") that brings awareness to the movement of *chi* or *qi* (life force), and what the Romans called *genius loci* (guardian spirit of place), the Hawaiians call *wahi pana* (sacred place) and it has to do with the *mana* (spiritual dynamics) of a location. Awakening our senses to the special qualities of a place, the wahi pana of the Hawaiian landscape, is what this guidebook hopes to encourage.

It is important for more people to find that archaeology, ancient art, ethnobotany, geography and geology, myths and legends, and even place names can add rich and enlivening dimensions to their understanding of Hawai'i. Reading cannot replace the experience of standing at a site and encountering with all one's senses the way a natural formation or an ancient construction is set within the elements. The way a heiau (temple) is carefully placed on a mountain ridge, or the manner in which a pōhaku (stone) declares its commitment to a particular location, can be experienced only through a visit to the site itself. The intention of a petroglyph image, or the structural gesture created by the water-embracing walls of a fishpond, read differently in nature than on the print of a page, because their art and mystery are not yet trapped and interpreted by the intellect. The late Edward Kanahele said: "These places possess spiritual power, mana, but the designation wahi pana means much more than just a sacred geographical spot. In Hawaiian culture, the idea of 'place' itself holds deep meaning." Just as each person is more than a physical body, so too a landscape has more to offer than just its physical attributes.

Most of the sites included in this book are sacred to the native Hawaiian people. The sites and their surroundings should be treated with respect; nothing should be removed or altered. In the case of heiau, which are sometimes burial places, rock walls and platforms should not be climbed or crossed unless an obvious path is provided. It is also important that visitors leave nothing that could have an impact on the feature or the environment. Again, Kanahele says: "If the visitor feels spiritually compelled to connect with a wahi pana then one should offer a ho'okupu [gift offering.] One of the ho'okupu of highest value in the native Hawaiian culture is not an offering of fruit or vegetables or foliage; neither is it an offering of a fish [or a stone wrapped in a ti leaf] or a whale's tooth or a family heirloom; rather it is one's word! One's commitment! One's promise! One's sincere oath to pay deference to and uphold the physical and spiritual values of the culture! One's word is the ho'okupu of choice!"

When first visiting a site, view it from a distance and consider the immediate impression it has upon you. What is the *feeling* of the place? Hold off judgments and simply be in awe, in openness, in wonder. Proceed up to and gradually move around the site and note its size, shape, material, and placement in the surroundings. Often only a pile of rocks is to be seen. Note the angle of the light and how the shadows fall. See how the landscape embraces the site. Consider the vegetation growing nearby. Remember that the light changes during the course of the day and the year, and a forested area may have been treeless a century or two ago just as a clearing may have been overgrown. Take in the views from various directions remembering many sites were oriented to certain stars or to sunrise and sunset. Not least of all, be conscious of your feelings (emotional intelligence or cognitive feeling should be engaged) as you actively appreciate the physical site and experience the *spirit of the place.*

Hawaiian ancient history is an important chapter in the history of humanity, and many of the sites illustrating this history are accessible. Ancient sites are markers in our present journey from past to future.

An attempt has been made with this book to bring together introductory background material concerning various island sites. Differing opinions among scholars, historians, current researchers, archaeologists, and Hawaiian practitioners, as well as oral traditions and legends, have been presented wherever possible to give as complete a picture as possible. However, this work is anything but exhaustive, for only a few of the numerous sites on Maui, Moloka'i and Lāna'i are mentioned here, and only the accessible ones. The intention is simply to introduce and guide readers to sites that are generally known and easily visited. In some cases, permission or an entrance fee is required, but in all cases the sites listed here are open to interested visitors.

Over time, many ancient sites in the Hawaiian Islands have been destroyed by natural forces, development, and vandalism. However, interest in saving ancient sites is strong and continues to grow. New sites are continually being discovered as development and preservation repeatedly confront one another and, at the best of times, work together. This book is intended to promote an appreciation and preservation of the ancient cultural sites of Maui, Moloka'i and Lāna'i so that not only our Hawaiian Islands but also our Earth-Island culture may rediscover and reawaken to the richness of our shared past in order to move with greater understanding and wisdom into the future.

—Van James
Honolulu, O'ahu, Hawai'i

ACKNOWLEDGMENTS

I would like to thank a number of people and organizations for helping me with various stages of the work on *Ancient Sites of Maui, Moloka'i and Lāna'i;* they include: Patrice Belcher, Pat Boland, Nickolai Browne, Christina Chang, Francis Cleland, Alice Cooper, Stacy Helm Crivello, Jocelyn Romero Demirbag, Linda Domen, Pat Finberg, Virginia Fish, Scott Fisher of Hawaiian Island Land Trust, Butch Haase of Moloka'i Land Trust, Kay Hirayama, Roy Ihara, Sam Ka'ai, Sol Kaho'ohalahala, the late John Ka'imikaua, Pi'ilani Lua, the late Richard Marks of Damein Tours and Rick Schonely, Keith and Lynette McCrary, Davianna McGregor, Clifford Nae'ole, Marie Place, Mike Opgenorth, Bob Ozaki, Terrence Ozaki, the late Nick Palumbo, George Reed, Kekai Robinson, "Junior" August Rollins, Patrick Ryan, Lei'ohu Ryder, Richard Schuman and Andy Yee of Makani Kai Air, Christi Shaw of the National Park Service, Pilipo and Greg Solatorio, Jack Spruance, Ellen Sugawara, Teri Waros, Viola Yee, Martha Yent of State Parks, Leina and Melse of the Hāna Cultural Center and Museum, Lea of the former Mānele Bay Hotel, and colleagues of the Honolulu Waldorf School and Haleakalā Waldorf School. Thanks to Bishop Museum Archive, the Bailey House Museum Archive and Hawai'i State Library.

Special acknowledgement goes to Kahu Kapiiohookalani Lyons Naone for his Foreword, the late Edward Kanahele for the ever-current Preface, to David L. Eyre for his attention to the Hawaiian language in this publication and his contribution on Hawaiian pronunciation, and to Cammy Doi for her help with early drafts. Many thanks to everyone at Mutual Publishing—Bennett, Jane, and Courtney—for putting this work together with such ease and interest.

As ever, mahalo nui loa to my wife Bonnie for her constant encouragement, support, and aloha.

HOW TO USE THIS BOOK

This guidebook begins with a brief survey of ancient Hawaiian culture and a description of the five major types of sites to be found on the islands of Maui, Moloka'i and Lāna'i. A map of each island's most accessible ancient sites is followed by descriptions, photographs, and detailed area maps.

The sites are grouped into regional districts, many of which are also the ancient land divisions. The sites of some districts can be viewed in one day of touring. In some cases the sites of two or more districts can be combined into one trip. However, to experience fully the natural and archaeological resources, several days' exploration would be ideal.

If you are visiting the Islands and have little time to explore, you might read the site descriptions first and then simply pick and choose those you wish to see. Appendix A: Selected Sites for Visitors offers some suggestions for first-time explorers.

The local site-seer has the advantage of time and can also make use of the "pick and choose" approach. Read the site descriptions and arrange your excursions as time and circumstances permit.

This book can also be used in such a way that, if you are interested in particular kinds of sites, such as petroglyphs, just consult the list at the end of the Types of Sites chapter. Then find your selection by title in the Site Location section.

Those interested in further information on ancient sites can consult the Bibliography at the back of the book. Following each site description you will find groups of numbers in parentheses. The first number, or number on its own, indicates a title in the Bibliography, and the second number refers to the page in that book, e.g. (13/25) is 13. James, V. 1998. *Ancient Sites of O'ahu*, page 25).

ANCIENT HAWAIIANS

ike most indigenous peoples, the ancient Hawaiians felt a deep connection with nature. They experienced the forces that caused thunder and lightning or created sunshine and rainbows to be the same elemental forces that allowed them to stand, to walk and to chant. These natural forces were so powerful and so alive to the ancient Hawaiians that they were called by name and recognized as beings. Thus, an entire pantheon of gods, goddesses, and demigods were associated with the elements of water, snow, clouds, and fire, and dwelt in fish, animals, plants, and other natural phenomena. The gods Kū, Kāne, Lono, the goddess Pele, and the demi-god Māui, are just a few of the supernatural beings remembered today in Hawaiʻi.

The ancient Hawaiian fisherman, kalo (taro) farmer, canoe builder, and kapa (cloth) maker were in constant conversation with nature and, thereby, in regular discourse with the gods. The soil, stones, plants, wood, wind, clouds, and light all expressed a meaning-filled content. For this reason, the ancient Hawaiians were sensitive to, and revered the world around, them. By reading the "Book of Nature," Hawaiians developed effective medical arts based entirely on natural remedies. Their knowledge also enabled them to develop and manage fishponds, some of the most advanced aquaculture in the world. This is not to say that

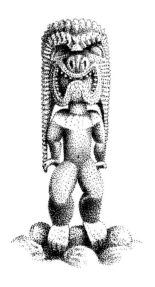

Kū, god of war, was usually depicted in a threatening pose with toothed grimace and flexed legs. Such akua kiʻi, (carved wooden images), stood within and sometimes along the approach to heiau (temple) precincts. These images embodied the mana (divine power) of certain gods and spirits; they were not seen as the gods themselves, but acted as channeling posts for divine powers. Few authentic akua kiʻi survived the purging of the old religion initiated by the aliʻi (chiefly class) themselves in their zeal as new converts to missionary teachings in the early nineteenth century. This particular image is an example of the late Kona-style wood sculpture and can be seen at the Bishop Museum in Honolulu.

the ancient Hawaiians had a perfect society without injustice, illness, or environmental destruction. However, in some respects their culture exemplified how a human community could be self-sufficient and enjoy a harmonious and mutually beneficial relationship with nature.

Myths and Legends

> *These are my gods, whom I worship. Whether I do right or*
> *wrong I do not know. But I follow my faith, which cannot*
> *be wicked, as it commands me never to do wrong.*
> —Kamehameha the Great

This intimate relationship to nature was expressed in lively, imaginative stories and passed on from one generation to the next in the form of chants, ka'ao (short stories) and mo'olelo (stories). Myths related accounts of the major gods and goddesses, while legends passed on the more localized tales, into which much of the cultural history of old Hawai'i was woven. In addition to the myths and legends, traditional history presented more factual accounts from the recent past. Meaning, morality, and spiritual values were an integral part of the mythological, legendary, and traditional histories. Such accounts demonstrated how the world arose as a result of creative spirit, how physical objects and facts were the results of godly deeds. In this sense, Pele, the volcano goddess, was seen as the inspirer of image-making in Hawai'i, perhaps because of the unending form possibilities that can be found in lava rock structures. The fiery, creative spirit Pele thus establishes herself as the first sculptor.

The Kapu System

> *Mālama o pā 'oe.*
> Be careful lest the result be disastrous to you.
> [Watch your step lest evil attach itself to you. A warning
> not to break a kapu.] (31/231)
> —Hawaiian saying

The social order of old Hawai'i rested on the principal of mana, the spiritual power that all things possess to a greater or lesser degree. Stones, plants, animals, people, and the gods all possess this vital force, according to the Hawaiians. In order to protect and revere this sacred mana, laws or kapu were established. These kapu set down strict societal "dos and don'ts" and the transgressor often paid with his or her life. Examples of important kapu were fishing out of season, stepping on the chief's shadow, and eating pig or certain kinds of bananas if you were a woman. Acquittal was possible for a kapu breaker if he or she could reach a pu'uhonua (place of refuge) and be cleansed and exonerated of the misdeed by a kahuna (priest). In times of war, the pu'uhonua was especially important as a refuge for warriors and women and children whose side had been defeated in battle.

The kapu system, as it is understood today, primarily maintained the power and authority of the ali'i, (chiefly class), within the social order. It was also instrumental in defining traditional beliefs and preserving ancient knowledge and customs.

The Ali'i

He 'ehu wāwae no kalani.
A trace of the heavenly one's footsteps.
[The rain, the rainbow, and other signs seen when a chief is abroad are tokens of his recognition by the gods.] (38/65)
—Hawaiian saying

The ali'i, (royal class), were at the pinnacle of the Hawaiian social order and kapu system. This highborn group possessed great mana and were therefore the rulers and leaders of the people. They were the heads of the community, the caretakers of their ancestors' memory, and the guardians of the gods on earth. Some ruled well, protecting their subjects from harm whenever possible; others ruled poorly, taking advantage of the kapu system and inflicting suffering for no apparent reason.

Kamehameha the Great (1758–1819) was perhaps the most powerful of the Hawaiian Island chiefs and is remembered by many as a wise and noble leader. An exceptional destiny was forecast for "the lonely one," who was born during the appearance of Halley's Comet. As a young man, he proved himself a fierce warrior in battle and, as another sign of his greatness, moved the legendary Naha stone in Hilo. His uncle, Chief Kalani'ōpu'u, appointed Kamehameha guardian of the family war god Kūkā'ilimoku ("Kū the land grabber"), and divided up the island of Hawai'i between his two sons Kīwala'ō and Keōua, Kamehameha's cousins. Kamehameha gained the Kona and Kohala districts of Hawai'i by defeating his elder cousin Kīwala'ō at the Battle of Moku'ōhai in 1782. He gained control over the rest of the Big Island in 1791, when he invited Keōua to the dedication of Pu'ukoholā Heiau, and offered him as the sacrifice. Kamehameha went on to conquer Maui, Moloka'i, Lāna'i, and O'ahu by 1795, reaching an agreement with Kaua'i in 1810 that made Kamehameha ruler of all the Hawaiian Islands. As the first chief to unite all of the Hawaiian Islands, he was also the first king. Shortly after his death the ancient kapu system collapsed when, in 1819, two of his wives, Ka'ahumanu, his favorite, and the highborn Keōpūolani, together with his son, Liholiho (Kamehameha II), abolished many of the old laws, as well as the traditional religious order.

Kamehameha the Great established the kingdom of Hawai'i by uniting all of the islands under his rule. His name means "the lonely one" or "the one alone." Ka'ahumanu, the favorite wife of Kamehameha, served as regent of Hawai'i after the king's
death in 1819 until her own death in 1832. She played an important part in the overthrow of the old kapu (sacred prohibition) system. (Ludwig Choris, 1816, Wikimedia
Commons)

The Kāhuna

> *Ko ke kahuna ha'i kupua.*
> To the kahuna belongs the duty of declaring the revela-
> tions of the supernatural beings. (31/196)
> — Hawaiian saying

Kamehameha and other powerful chiefs had kāhuna (priests or specialists), who served as their advisors. These kāhuna were not only spiritual counselors, but political advisors, as well. Particularly skilled kāhuna often provided needed guidance and direction for the ali'i.

Hawaiian oral tradition speaks of Pā'ao, a light-skinned kahuna
who came to the Islands sometime between the tenth and thirteenth
centuries from Kahiki. (Some sources suggest that Kahiki refers to Tahiti, Samoa Society Islands, or the Marquesas.) Arriving on the Big Island of Hawai'i, Pā'ao overthrew the harsh Big Island chief, Kamaiole,
and sent for a suitable ali'i from his homeland to be installed as the
new high chief. Pili Ka'ai'ea was brought to Hawai'i, establishing a new
royal line that would lay the foundations for later rulers such as those
of the Kamehameha lineage. A strong kapu system seems to have been

emphasized at this time, along with the practice of human sacrifice. Pā'ao is also credited with encouraging the carving of wooden ki'i, (images), for religious purposes, and the building of more elaborate heiau than had previously been constructed.

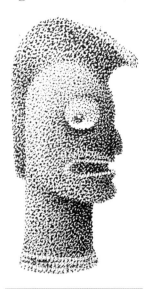

Kāhuna were not always spiritual or political advisors. A kahuna was, in fact, anyone who was expert in a particular field. Healers, artists, craftspersons, even master farmers and fishermen could be kāhuna. Long training was required of the apprentice kahuna before he or she gained the knowledge and discipline to become kahuna lapa'au (medical practitioner), kahuna kālai (master carver), kahuna hana 'upena (master fishnet maker), or kahuna ho'oulu 'ai (agricultural expert). Such skills were passed from one generation to another, from teacher to pupil, through hands-on, repetitive practice, often from a young age. No texts, scores, or written notations helped the haku mele (master of chants and music) learn to recall and chant the thousands of lines of verse required to preserve the oral history. No compass, charts, or sextant aided the kahuna ho'okele (navigator), and, yet, by reading the sizes, shapes and colors of clouds, the wave movements, flights of birds, currents, and stars, this kahuna learned to guide his voyaging canoe over thousands of sea miles, an accomplishment doubted in the West until only recently. The disciplines developed by the kahuna class clearly demonstrate a civilization, which, although not technologically advanced in a modern sense, displayed a high achievement in cultural life and human capabilities.

Kūka'ilimoku, "the land grabber," was an embodiment of the major god Kū and a god of war to whom numan sacrifices were offered. Kamehameha the Great was a guardian of the 'aumakua hulu manu (feathered god image) of Kūka'ilimoku and he invoked this god in order to conquer Hawai'i Island, Maui, Moloka'i, Lana'i, and O'ahu.

Ancient Sites

The kāhuna, the ali'i, and the commoners made appropriate offerings to their 'aumākua (ancestral spirits) and their gods. For such worship, they erected sacred pōhaku (stones), shrines, and heiau (temples). These ancient Hawaiian religious sites, together with petroglyphs and the remnants of fishponds, are but the bare bones of a once flourishing civilization. Yet, these remains from the archaeological record, in conjunction with myths, legends, and traditional history, provide us with a glimpse into the rich cultural life of old Hawai'i.

Most of the sites listed in this book are several hundred years old. As dating methods improve and new sites are discovered, the accepted time of settlement of the Hawaiian Islands continues to recede. The latest estimates now point to about the second or third century. However, neither dating techniques nor the archaeological reconstructions of ancient sites are exact and final, as conclusions based on limited evidence are usually involved. What we may consider true today is not often what many thought was true yesterday nor what will likely be seen as true tomorrow.

This guide to the ancient sites of Hawai'i deals only with heiau (temples), pōhaku (stones), ki'i pōhaku (petroglyphs), caves and fishponds of Maui, Moloka'i and Lāna'i. Other features mentioned only in passing include house sites, animal pens, walls, agricultural terraces, battlefields, irrigation ditches, wells, salt pans, paths and roadways, hōlua (sled) courses, and pu'uhonua (places of refuge). These latter features should not be considered of lesser importance, for they all contribute to a more comprehensive understanding of ancient Hawaiian culture and the spirit of place, or wahi pana. (1; 13; 14; 15; 16; 17; 20; 22; 25; 32; 39)

> *E hiolo ana nā kapu kahiko;*
> *e hina ana nā heiau me nā lele;*
> *e hui ana nā moku;*
> *he iho mai ana ka lani a e pi'i ana ka hōnua.*
> The ancient kapu will be abolished;
> the heiau and altars will fall;
> the islands will be united;
> the heavens will descend and the earth ascend.
> [A prophecy uttered by Kapihe, a kahuna in Kamehameha's time. The last part of the saying means that chiefs will come down to humble positions and commoners rise to positions of honor.] (31/35)
>
> —Hawaiian saying

TYPES OF SITES

Heiau (Temples) and Shrines

A heiau is a Hawaiian temple, a place of worship, offering and sacrifice. The heiau is one of the most endur-  ing architectural forms from pre-historic Hawai'i, but it is also the most important architectural form from the perspective of Hawaiian religion. As with most ancient civilizations, the temple architecture represents and expresses the culture. With an intense and immediate experience of the forces in nature and an intuitive relationship with their gods, the ancient Hawaiians looked to the heiau and their kāhuna (priests) for order, understanding, and guidance in the ways of the universe. This was the case as well with practical everyday matters such as ascertaining the times for planting and harvesting, fishing and refraining from fishing, healing illness and mending broken bones. Even giving thanks and being at peace with one's neighbors or going to war and taking another's life were connected with the role of the kāhuna and the heiau.

The kahuna was responsible to the people as a mediator with the gods. Many chiefs had a kahuna to consult, particularly on questions dealing with the maintenance of power, and the heiau was the main center for kāhuna activity.

According to oral tradition, Pā'ao was the first priest to bring from Kahiki a new religious impulse promoting and establishing a severe kapu (taboo) system. Some researchers believe that during his era, human sacrifice in connection with the worship of Kū superseded a more peaceful form of religious practice that centered on the god Kāne. Pā'ao is said to be the kahuna kuhikuhipu'uone, or architect, behind the tenth to thirteenth century Waha'ula Heiau, as well as the Mo'okini Heiau on the island of Hawai'i, both of which were of the luakini (human sacrifice) type.

Lono, god of agriculture, fertility, and peace, along with Kū, was already revered in Hawai'i at the time of the arrival of Pā'ao. Kāne, a god of freshwater sources, and Kanaloa, god of the ocean, along with numerous other gods and goddesses, were also worshipped at heiau throughout the Islands.

The line of Big Island chiefs, leading down to Kamehameha the Great, seems to have stressed and ultimately spread a preference for Lono and the aggressive Kū over the other gods. It has been suggested that Kāne, god of flowing water and kalo (taro) production, may have been more important on Maui and Moloka'i, where some heiau are oriented toward his direction, the East. Haleki'i and Pihanakalani Heiau in Wailuku, Maui, are believed to have originally honored more peaceful gods during the early period but later revered more aggressive gods, as the heiau were physically reoriented to face Hawai'i island at a time when Maui was in a warring relationship with its neighbor.

Only paramount chiefs, through their kāhuna, could consecrate heiau of the lua-kini type, where human sacrifices ensuring political power and preserving mana (spiritual power) were carried out. The preferred human sacrifice was a captive enemy, a warrior with much mana, ali'i having the greatest mana. A criminal was a lesser sacrifice, and the lowest grade was a kauā (outcast), a person considered to have little mana and capable of robbing mana from others.

Pi'ilanihale Heiau in Hana is the largest surviving place of ancient ritual practice on the island of Maui. Located in Hana it has a remarkably high, terraced wall construction and spectacular coastal view.

Human sacrifice occurred late in the development of many ancient civilizations, and it has been suggested that such practices may have been adopted in order to maintain a "fresh" connection to the spirit world at a time when spiritual vision was failing. However, scholars today generally consider human sacrifice as a symbolic death and rebirth of the chief, for the purpose of maintaining and renewing the social order. Human sacrifice was the ultimate offering to the gods, petitioning them to preserve and revitalize society.

Although human sacrifice figured in only a small part of the religious practices of the ancient Hawaiians, the heiau luakini are nevertheless quite numerous and usually larger in size than other types of temples. This seems due, in part, to the tradition that only a few paramount chiefs held the privilege of establishing and using luakini, and they did this to assert their power and demonstrate their prestige. (However, by the time temple functions were recorded, the term luakini

Hale o Keawe Heiau at Puʻuhonua o Hōnaunau on the island of Hawaiʻi has been re-constructed in the last century to resemble the way it looked in ancient times.

meant "religious place" and was applied even to Christian churches.) Piʻilanihale Heiau in East Maui and ʻIliʻiliʻōpae Heiau on Molokaʻi are important heiau luakini.

Most heiau, apart from the luakini, could be dedicated by lesser chiefs. Some of these other heiau were the husbandry type, sometimes called Hale o Lono, where the promotion and increase of livestock and agriculture were fostered. The heiau hoʻoulu ʻai were devoted to insure good fishing. Heiau maʻo were designed to promote an abundance of food. Heiau hoʻo ulu ua were where offerings were made to promote rain. Typical offerings at such heiau were pigs, bananas, and coconuts.

At a less common type of heiau, healers known as kāhuna lapaʻau, were trained in the ancient art of medicine. Herbal remedies and spiritual healing were practiced at sacred sites throughout Hawaiʻi, and the surroundings of these heiau served as the natural pharmacy for plant remedies of all kinds. Keaīwa Heiau on Oʻahu is the best-known site of this kind.

Heiau were not just places of ritual offering and sacrifice but also places for priestly observation of the starry heavens, the weather, and the changes in the nature. Some heiau were quickly constructed over a few-day period, used to fulfill a specific need, and then abandoned. Sites were reused only when the need arose.

No two heiau seem to have been constructed in the same way as far as ground plans are concerned. Though often built on a rectangular rock platform, some heiau were terraced or stepped with one or more levels, while others had walled enclosures. Professor of archaeology Patrick Kirch categorizes heiau forms as follows: notched, square, elongated double-court, platform or terrace, and irregular. In addition there can be the koʻa fishing shrines, agricultural shrines, pōhaku o Kāne, and other types of shrines. Kirch also maintains: "These enclosures can be distinguished from house sites by their larger size, better-constructed walls (usually incorporating large boulders in the base course, and often upright slabs as well), cardinal wall orientations, and often presence of branch coral offerings." (23/174)

Wooden fences often surrounded the temple precinct and grass hale (houses) stood within the enclosure, but none of these features has survived. However, at some sites, such as Ahuʻena Heiau in Kailua-Kona and Hale o Keawe Heiau at Puʻuhonua o Hōnaunau in South Kona on the Big Island, these perishable structures have been reconstructed. In most cases, stone foundations are the only part of these temples that we see today.

One of the hale within the heiau precinct would have been the hale mana (house of spiritual power or the house of the resident god). Sometimes a hale pahu (drum house), a wai ea (small house where incantations were invoked), and an oven house were also present. Wickerwork structures covered with tapa were where the kāhuna climbed inside to receive visions or messages from the gods. Called the ʻanuʻu

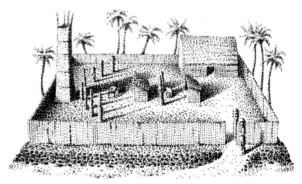

Typical features of the luakini (human sacrifice) heiau were, from left to right, the ʻanuʻu (oracle tower), which was entered only by the kāhuna; akua kiʻi (wooden images of the gods/ancestors); the lele (altar) for offerings; the hale pahu (drum house); more akua kiʻi; the hale wai ea (house of the ceremonial ʻaha cord); the oven house; the hale mana (house of spiritual power) for the aliʻi; and more images at the precinct entrance.

(tower), these vertical enclosures are also referred to as oracle towers, and stood near the lele (altar). Akua kiʻi (sacred wooden images) guarded the entrance to the compound and watched over the altar. Although burials have been found within heiau precincts, a heiau should not be thought of as a cemetery in the contemporary sense. Burials were likely aids for a kahuna in his practice as a mediator between this world and the other, and were sometimes temporary until a more appropriate cave or burial site could be found.

Not a great deal is understood about the actual heiau rituals, as they were already being abandoned as foreign settlers arrived in the early nineteenth century. However, one source is Captain James Cook's journals wherein he describes heiau ceremonies that he observed during his visit to the Hawaiian Islands in the late eighteenth century.

Describing the human sacrifice at the heiau luakini, Samuel Kamakau, one of the Native Hawaiian authorities writing in the mid-nineteenth century, said the dead person was reddened over a fire and placed face down with his right arm over a pig offering and his left hand holding a bunch of bananas. The high chief, or mōʻī, then pierced the mouth of the dead man with a ceremonial hook called the mānaiakalani, and recited the following words:

> *E Kū, e Lono,*
> *E Kāne, e Kanaloa,*
> *E ola iaʻu a kau i ka puaneane;*
> *E nānā i ke kipi ʻāina,*
> *I ka lelemū o.*
> *ʻĀmama. Ua noa.*

> O Kū, o Lono,
> O Kāne and Kanaloa,
> Give life to me until my old age;
> Look at the rebel against the land,
> He who was seized for sacrifice.
> Finished. [It is freed of the kapu]. (16/130)

The kahuna nui also recited a prayer and those assembled listened for the sound of a bird, lizard, or rat, a sign that the sacrifice had been accepted.

A special type of sacred area was the puʻuhonua, a place of refuge and forgiveness for kapu breakers. Every island had several such protected areas for the absolution of lawbreakers. The most famous of these is Puʻuhonua o Hōnaunau, in Kona, on the Big Island. Halulu Heiau at Kaunolū, Lānaʻi, is also a puʻuhonua.

The smaller, common places of worship were the koʻa (fishing), roadside ahu and boundary shrines. These shrines were numerous throughout the Islands and sometimes consisted of a single upright pōhaku (stone), or perhaps a rock structure the size of a small heiau. They might be dedicated to a ʻaumakua (family god) or one of the many lesser Hawaiian gods or goddesses.

Koʻa were an important type of small shrine, and remained in use long after the more formal heiau functions ceased in Hawaiʻi. Fishermen offered their first catch at such shrines, which were usually located near the water and dedicated to the diety Kūʻula. Koʻa were sacred to specific fish and were known to attract certain species. A koʻa might be one or more stones, naturally situated or artificially placed, often having a smooth upright stone representing Kūʻula. Such sites, as well as many heiau, usually contained bits of white branch coral, even if the

As places of ritual practice, heiau can be large stonewalled enclosures or terraced platforms but can also be a simple ahu or shrine-like structure, as this one on Maui, or even a single upright stone.

sites were located a great distance from the ocean. Koʻa means "coral" or "coral head."

It is believed that family shrines dedicated to the ʻaumākua were an important part of every household. These shrines took the form of a single stone figure or an altar made up of many stones. Sometimes a special grass hale was built to house the ʻaumākua; otherwise, the akua stood in the common living quarters or just outside in the open.

Road shrines often marked the boundary between one ahupuaʻa (land division or district) and another. There, travelers may have made offerings for a safe journey or left district tax payments, as was the custom. Today it is often difficult to imagine that a shrine, a sacred site, could be as simple as a single pōhaku (stone).

Please remember to respect all heiau just as you would a church, temple, or any other sacred site. (7; 13; 15; 16; 21; 23; 39)

Heiau List:

Waiheʻe Coastal Dunes and Wetlands Refuge, Kealakaʻihonua Heiau, Wailuku, Maui
Halekiʻi and Pihanakalani Heiau, Wailuku, Maui
Kaukealiʻi Heiau, Waiʻānapanapa (State Park), Hāna, Maui
Piʻilanihale Heiau, Hāna, Maui
ʻIliʻiliʻōpae Heiau, Molokaʻi
Kalaupapa, Molokaʻi
Halulu Heiau, Kaunolū, Lānaʻi

Pōhaku (Sacred Stones)

Many of the prominent stones and distinctive rock formations in Hawai'i are sacred sites. Usually these sites have their own names and are featured in myths and legends. According to tradition, some represent individuals transformed into stone, while others serve as dwelling places for specific spirit beings or gods. Pōhaku Wahine Pe'e on Maui and Pu'u Pehe on Lāna'i are examples.

The pōhaku (stone), whether it was a small 'ili'ili (pebble) or a megalithic pali (cliff), played a very significant part in the life of ancient Hawai'i. The features of the land spoke to the early Hawaiians in an imaginative pictorial language and, therefore, many rocks and stones possessed distinctive characters and individual names. The phallic rock, Kauleonānāhoa, on Moloka'i is just such a stone with its own fascinating story.

Kauleonānāhoa, a phallic rock on a hillside in upcountry Moloka'i, is an ancient fertility site where women wishing to become pregnant would make offerings and spend the night.

Gifts for the local deity were often left at pōhaku sites. Various forms of ancestral worship were also celebrated at these sites, especially when the stones also marked burial places. However, pōhaku did not serve merely as gravestones in a conventional sense, rather they were altar-like monuments indicating where an ancestor could be contacted. Some stones were used by the kāhuna during spiritual practices, and others served as boundary markers for land divisions or districts. Seen in this way, a pōhaku stood in the landscape as a physical reminder of a spiritual threshold. These sites were places where one could commune with the gods. In some cases, these rock sites were "jumping off" places where the souls of the dead entered the other world. Pu'u Keka'a, on Maui's west coast, is such a place.

Still other pōhaku were known as ko'a (fishing shrines) and were used to locate favorite fishing grounds. The first catch of the day was left at the ko'a as an offering of thanks to the god or goddess. A kū'ula was generally a medium-sized stone housing a spirit helpful to fishermen.

This pōhaku was struck with a stick in ancient times in order to create a ringing tone that could be heard throughout the area. Such bellstones as Pōhaku o Kani can also be found on other islands in Hawai'i.

Often speaking through a dream, a kū'ula could direct a fisherman to the stone's location and then, if properly cared for, might reward the fisherman with good fishing and a healthy life. Kū'ula is the name of an important fish god (see site V.28).

Some stones were named after the fish, animals, or objects that their shapes suggested. Sometimes called Pōhaku o Kāne, they were often used as household shrines. Jagged and porous stones were considered female, while smooth, fine-grained stones were thought of as male. Usually, light stones were female and dark-colored ones, male. Healing stones such as Pōhaku Hauola in Lahaina, Maui, were also important to ancient Hawaiians.

In ancient times, Hawaiians would leave fist-sized stones on top of ti leaf offerings in order to prevent the leaf from blowing away. The strictly modern practice of wrapping a specially chosen stone in a ti leaf has evolved from the older tradition. (10; 13; 14; 20; 24; 37)

A large hoana pōhaku or adze grinding stone is on the grounds of the Bailey House Museum in Wailuku, Maui.

> *He Ola Ka Pōhaku.*
> There is Life in the Stone.
>
> —Hawaiian saying

Pōhaku Sites:

Kapalua, Lahaina, Maui
Pu'u Keka'a, Lahaina, Maui
Pōhaku Moemoe and Wahine Pe'e, Lahaina, Maui
Pōhaku Hauola, Lahaina, Maui
Pōhaku O Mā'alaea, Wailuku, Maui
Kēkaemoku, 'Īao Valley, Wailuku, Maui
Ka Iwi O Pele, Hāna, Maui
Ka'uiki Head, Hāna, Maui
Wai'ānapanapa (State Park), Hāna, Maui
Pōhaku Hāwanawana, Moloka'i
Kalama'ula, Moloka'i
Pāpōhaku, Moloka'i
Kauleonānāhoa, Moloka'i
Keahiakawelo, Lāna'i
Pu'u Pehe, Lāna'i

Ki'i Pōhaku (Petroglyphs)

Petroglyphs (petro = stone, glyph = writing), or ki'i pōhaku, are pictures, words or letters, carved into rock surfaces—images engraved in stone.

Hawaiian petroglyphs remained simple in style and imagery, even after contact with European explorers, whalers, and missionaries. According to early authorities, Hawaiian petroglyphs did not have great cultic or religious significance beyond celebrating personal experiences or acknowledging the 'aumākua. However, even with this more limited application in terms of religious expression, the creating of ki'i pōhaku was nevertheless a sacred craft, as were the even more practical activities of weaving, wood carving, tattooing, and tapa design. Stylized petroglyphs and the geometric designs of tattoos and tapa cloth represent some of the high points in the development of ancient Hawaiian two-dimensional visual arts, and a reevaluation of their significance is ongoing.

Petroglyphs appear at well over 150 known sites in the Hawaiian Islands, and most of those sites are on the Big Island. The forms in these stone carvings are dots or cup marks, circles, straight lines, wavy and curved lines, as well as simple stick figures denoting dogs, turtles, birds, pigs, crabs, and human beings. Early Hawaiians drew anthropomorphic (human-animal) figures, the most well known being the birdman figures that appear on several of the Hawaiian Islands. Men on surfboards and canoe paddlers with paddles in hand are also represented, along with sails, kites, and canoes. Post-contact petroglyphs depict Western ships, horse-

Some of the animals depicted in petroglyphs include the dog, pig, chicken, bird, turtle, and crab. Animals were often 'aumākua (guardian spirits) for Hawaiian families.

back riders, and Hawaiian words (writing was introduced in the 1820s by missionaries).

Four different techniques are used in creating petroglyphs. These vary with the sharpness of the artist's stone tools. Sharp adzes produced pecked and incised designs; duller tools created bruised and abraded designs. Metal tools were sometimes used in post-contact times.

Petroglyphs may indicate the boundary of a district or ahupua'a (land division). Many cultures worldwide have used markings of some kind at territorial borders. Ancient travelers were sometimes called upon to contribute to these sites by adding a stone or carving a figure as an offering.

Most of the Hawaiian petroglyphs were carved in smooth pāhoehoe (lava rock), which provided a good surface for images. Some are even found in lava-tube caves. However, ki'i pōhaku were also carved on the faces of large stream boulders and on coralline sandstone ledges along the older geological coastal structures. All of the petroglyph sites mentioned here utilize boulders or smooth basalt rock surfaces, as opposed to the abundant lava rock that is used on the Big Island.

Unique to East Maui are pictographs, painted images on stone. Painted with red ochre pigments, or kukui nut dye, these works are very rare but can still be found in the Makawao and Hāna districts. The single image at Wai'ānapanapa is the only one on accessible land.

Some of the Hawaiian rock art images are related to local mythology, while

Pictographs, paintings on stone, are found only in Hawai'i on East Maui and Lāna'i. This human figure with two turtle images is located in a Kula upcountry gulch on private land. It was painted with red ochre, or kukui nut dye.

others may depict pre-contact and early historic events. Some of the cup-mark, or piko (belly button), circle petroglyphs are connected with a birth ritual of placing the umbilical cord stump of a newborn child in a carved lua (indentation) and covering it with a stone. In this way the child was believed to receive mana (spiritual power) from the cosmos.

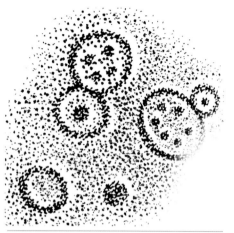

The stone covering prevented rats from stealing the piko stump. A thief in Hawaiian is referred to as piko pau'iole. Of course, some images may have more than one meaning.

Hawaiian petroglyphs are not realistic renderings of nature, but stylized, symbolic images of forces and beings. Figures are not depicted within a physical space; there is no ground line, no background, and, therefore, no foreshortening, perspective, or depth. The differing sizes of figures may indicate rank or social status, as much as age and physical stature. Groupings of figures can be difficult to read as compositions because the various images may have been carved at different times and for different reasons. Where a cluster of figures occurs in a petroglyph field, the images at the center are gen-

Many petroglyph images are of dots and circles. The dot, a puka or lua (indentation), was, according to tradition, a receptacle for the newborn child's piko (umbilical cord stump). The dot within a circle is thought to be for the first-born of an ali'i family, and the circle alone is thought to be an 'umeke (calabash) awaiting the piko of the new child.

erally understood to be the oldest, with later carvings taking whatever smooth surface area remains at the periphery.

The best time to view petroglyphs is in the early morning or late afternoon when the sun is low in the sky. Petroglyphs are often difficult to see at midday because little or no shadow is cast in the shallow carved image area. For the best photographic results, stand with your back to the sun.

People have tried various methods of reproducing petroglyphs over the years, but such techniques as rubbing and casting damage rock art. The only safe method of reproducing petroglyph designs is to photograph or to make interpretive drawings of them. Do not try to enhance petroglyph images by recarving or even chalking them. Avoid walking on image areas and stay on viewing platforms where they are provided. Please protect all petroglyph sites! (6; 9; 10; 13; 20; 21; 24; 28; 37; 38; 40)

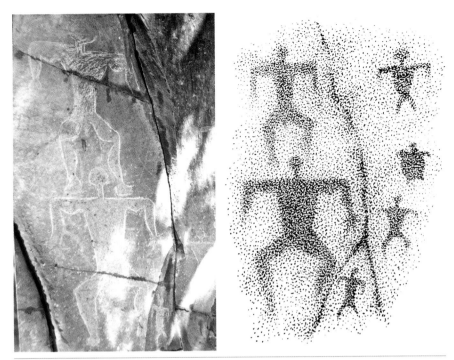

Human figures are regularly featured at the eighteen known petroglyph sites on Maui. These kiʻi pōhaku, located on private land in the southeastern region of Maui, also feature turtles.

Kiʻi Pōhaku Sites:

Olowalu, Lahaina, Maui
Nuʻu Landing, Hāna, Maui
Waiʻānapanapa (State Park), Hāna, Maui
Kawela Battleground, Molokaʻi
Kauleonānāhoa, Molokaʻi
Pōʻāiwa Petroglyphs, Lānaʻi
Kaunolū, Lānaʻi
Luahiwa Petroglyphs, Lānaʻi

Caves

The early Hawaiians used natural caves, lava tubes, and cliff overhangs as temporary shelters and places of refuge. Fishermen often took shelter from the weather in caves and bluff shelters close to the sea, as archaeological evidence such as fishhooks and marine artifacts indicates. Warriors used lava-tube caves, some of which extended from the sea to the mountains, for hiding from enemies and for waiting in ambush. Some caves were used as temporary homes, and still others served as dwelling places of one or more gods, and thus were kapu.

Burial caves were also kapu and were fairly numerous, used by aliʻi and commoners alike. Such caves provided ideal sites for laying the dead to rest and for seeking communion with ancestral spirits. Caves offer space withdrawn from the outer world; an inner space, quiet, dark, and protected. In some Hawaiian caves, the bones of the dead were placed in canoes to carry them on their voyage into the next world.

Most of the archaeologically important caves and lava tubes of Maui, Molokaʻi and Lānaʻi are not included here as site locations because of the need to protect them. Many of these sites have not been excavated and others are on private land that should not be trespassed. Most importantly, these are the sacred resting places of Native Hawaiians, and they should not be disturbed or violated. State and federal law protect all Hawaiian burials.

The only easily accessible cave mentioned here is the legendary lava tube hideaway of princess Pōpōʻalaea at Waiʻānapanapa State Park in Hāna, Maui. (9; 13; 20; 27; 37; 40)

Caves and rock shelters were used as burial places by ancient Hawaiians. Sometimes burials were committed to canoes and then secretly placed in a cave for the soul's journey into the other world after death. All burial sites are kapu and strictly off-limits to visitors. This is a cave shelter at Nuʻu on Maui.

Caves are generally off-limits in Hawai'i because they often serve as burial sites even to this day. However, some, like the cave at Wai'ānapanapa, may be visited.

> *'A'ohe e nalo ka iwi o ke ali'i 'ino,*
> *o ko ke ali'i maika'i ke nalo.*
> The bones of an evil chief will not be concealed,
> but the bones of a good chief will.
> [When an evil chief died, the people did not take
> the trouble to conceal his bones.] (31/17)
> —Hawaiian saying

Cave Sites:

Haleakalā, Maui
Nu'u Landing, Hāna, Maui
Ka'uiki Head, Hāna, Maui
Wai'ānapanapa (State Park),
    Hāna, Maui

Some ancient caves contained canoes with bone-bundles in them, intended to carry the deceased into the after-life.

Fishponds

Overseen by the fish god, Kū'ula, the activity of fishing was one of the most important ancient Hawaiian livelihoods. Besides shoreline fishing along the rugged coast and open-sea fishing from canoes, the Hawaiians developed a very sophisticated aquaculture system using fishponds. Though many ponds have been destroyed and only a very few are still operational, in recent years a lively interest has grown in rediscovering, restoring, and developing this ancient Hawaiian industry.

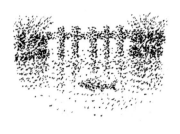

Hawaiian fishponds are unique in their design and construction. Nowhere else in the Pacific has such an efficient, practical, and productive system of aquaculture been developed. Evidence exists that fishponds were in use around 1200, which suggests their origin and development must be even earlier.

Most fishponds contained salt water or brackish water, but there were also freshwater ponds fed by streams and springs. Ponds had lanes or causeways to allow water in and out, and often mākāhā (wooden sluice gates) were employed. The mākāhā was designed to let small fish in to feed but to prevent them, once well fed and fat, from getting out. 'Anae (mullet), awa (milkfish), and āholehole (silver perch) were commonly stocked in Hawaiian fishponds.

There are five different types of fishponds: loko i'a kalo, loko wai, loko pu'uone, loko kuapā, and loko 'ume iki.

The loko 'ume iki is a large walled fishtrap, as opposed to an actual pond. Built out in the ocean along the reef, loko 'ume iki usually had several langes, or openings, leading into or out of the enclosure. The fish would then be netted from the lange. 'Ume iki means to "draw" or "attract," which is just what these loko (ponds) did. The loko 'ume iki are found only on the islands of Moloka'i and Lāna'i.

Loko kuapā means "walled pond," and these were often built of coral or basalt rock in shallow waters protected by reefs. Construction required a great deal of labor to pass large stones hand-to-hand over several miles. The walled enclosure often utilized a bay or cove and was loosely constructed, allowing water seepage to prevent stagnation within the pond. However, some loko kuapā have compact, dirt-filled walls. Mākāhā connected the pond directly with the ocean. Many of the fishponds on Moloka'i are loko kuapā.

Some of the Maui fishponds are of the loko pu'uone type, which means they are separated from the sea by a sand dune or earthen mound. These brackish ponds were connected to the ocean by lanes or streams, and mākāhā regulated water circulation and aided in harvesting the fish. The loko pu'uone were stream or spring fed, or both, and

The sluice gate of the Hawaiian fishpond is called a mākāhā. It lets seawater as well as small fish into the pond, but, once fish grow fat from feeding inside the pond, they can't get through the narrow openings.

the water level fluctuated with the rising and falling of the tides. Keālia Pond on Maui is an example of the loko puʻuone.

Loko wai were freshwater ponds, created by diverting a stream into a natural depression. These fishponds were generally small in size and, through a buildup of nutrients and freshwater algae, would turn green or brown in color. The loko wai was not directly connected to the sea.

Another inland pond was the loko iʻa kalo. Loko means pond, iʻa means fish, and kalo means taro. Loko iʻa kalo were taro fishponds stocked with fish. Taro, a main staple of the Hawaiians, was planted in flooded freshwater pond fields or channels, where āholehole (silver perch), ʻanae (mullet), awa (milkfish), ʻoʻopu (gobies), and ʻōpaeʻoehaʻa (clawed shrimp) fed around the ripening stalks. The loko iʻa kalo demonstrates a sophisticated system of integrated aquaculture and agriculture developed by the ancient Hawaiians.

Most fishponds belonged to the aliʻi, though some smaller ponds were used by commoners. A konohiki (headman) oversaw the ponds belonging to royalty, and called upon the people for any maintenance required. Everyone tended the fishponds until the kapu system was overthrown in 1819, the aliʻi gradually lost their power, and widespread disruption in lifestyle took place. As foreign diseases were introduced and the native Hawaiian population dwindled, trade patterns changed, and expertise in the construction and management of fishponds was lost.

There are some 488 fishponds, large and small, in varying states of disrepair throughout the Hawaiian Islands, 73 along a 40-mile stretch of Molokaʻi's south shore. If you keep a sharp eye out as you explore coastal areas, you will likely spot the remnants of old fishponds, signs of a unique ancient Hawaiian industry. (9; 13; 19; 20; 33; 35; 37; 41)

A number of fishponds on Moloka'i have been restored to their near-original condition.
This walled pond stretches out into shallow water on Moloka'i's southeastern shore.

> *Fishponds were things that beautified the land,*
> *and a land with many fishponds was called "fat."*
> —Samuel M. Kamakau

Fishpond Sites:

Kanahā Pond (State Wildlife Sanctuary), Wailuku, Maui
Keālia Pond (National Wildlife Refuge), Wailuku, Maui
Kō'ie'ie Fishpond, Wailuku, Maui
Haneo'o and Kaumaka Fishponds, Hāna, Maui
Southshore Fishponds, Moloka'i
Waia'ōpae Fishpond, Lāna'i
Naha Fishpond and Trail, Lāna'i

MAP OF THE ISLANDS

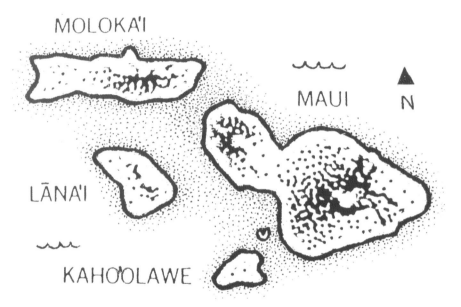

MOLOKA'I

MAUI

N

LĀNA'I

KAHO'OLAWE

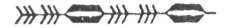

ANCIENT SITES OF MAUI

The island of Maui is the namesake of legendary Polynesian demigod Māui, son of Wākea and Papa. (Wākea was the primal male god; ākea is breadth, length, height, and depth of space. Papa was the primary female deity and the word papa means platform, reef, place to stand, and live.) Many places in Hawaiʻi and throughout Polynesia are remembered as locations where Māui fulfilled some miraculous feat or carried out a mischievous deed. His adventures proceed as far across the Pacific as Aeteora (New Zealand). However, it is the Valley Isle that is especially regarded as the site of this mythic hero's greatest adventures. Older names for the island of Maui are Ihikapalaumaewa and Kūlua.

The island is the second largest of the Hawaiian Islands, 48 miles long and 26 miles wide, formed from the remnants of two massive volcanic mountains. The West Maui Mountains or Mauna Kahalawai Range, referred to in oral tradition as Halemahina ("house of the moon") and featuring dramatic ʻIao Valley, is joined to the great dormant volcano, Haleakalā ("house of the sun"), by an isthmus known as the Central Valley. The deeply eroded, crescent-shaped West Maui Mountains peak at 5,788 feet on Puʻu Kukui, while the summit of Haleakalā reaches a height of 10,023 feet at Puʻu ʻUlaʻula and can be dusted with snow in the winter months. Mature coral reefs occur in places around 2 million year old West Maui but not around 400,000 year old East Maui.

Present day land divisions are closely based on ancient boundaries, with a few exceptions, and combine the island's twelve traditional moku (land divisions) into four large land areas. These larger districts are: I. Lahaina, which includes the entire leeward coast and most of the West Maui Mountains, the land sections of Lahaina and Kāʻanapali; II. Wailuku, which encompasses the Central Valley, ʻIao Valley, and the ahupuaʻa of Kīhei; III. Makawao, which includes the southern region of Maui, Honuaʻula, and the western slopes of Haleakalā, Kula, Hāmākuapoko, and Hāmākualoa; and IV. Hāna District, which is all of East Maui from the windward rim of Haleakalā to the sea, including the moku of Koʻolau, Hāna, Kīpahulu, Kaupō, and Kahikinui land sections. Each moku is divided into smaller upcountry to ocean land sections called ahupuaʻa, and even subdivided further into ʻili and moʻo.

Ancient cultural and political traditions group the islands of Molo-

The West Maui Mountains, or Halemahina ("house of the moon"), as seen from Lahaina's sacred Moku'ula and Loko Mokuhinia, now a public park.

ka'i, Lāna'i, and Kaho'olawe together with Maui. One tradition names Kaho'olawe as a leeward district of Maui and has therefore been included as one of the Maui sites (site 21). Today these islands, with the exception of Kaho'olawe, are all part of Maui County. Kaho'olawe was administered for many years by the U.S. Navy, which carried out live fire exercises on the island. Kaho'olawe was turned over to the State of Hawai'i and designated as a National Historical District in 1982 after years of protest and negotiation.

Paumakua is the name of the first known paramount chief, or mō'ī, of Maui. It is chanted that he was the 31st generation after Wakea. However, he and all the mō'ī that followed him only reigned over West Maui. That is until Pi'ilani, the 15th mō'ī, who was able to unite both sides of the island under his rule. From Pi'ilani around 1570, the high chiefs or kings of Maui have been Kiha a Pi'ilani (c.1590), Kamalālāwala (c.1610), Kauhi a Kama (c.1630), Kalanikaumakaōwakea (c.1650), Lonohonuakini (c.1670), Ka'ulahea II (c.1690), Kekaulike (c.1710), Kamehamehanui (c.1730), and Kahekili (c.1750). Kahekili II, the 25th high chief, conquered Moloka'i and O'ahu in 1783, and by marriage of his brother to Kaua'i's queen, expanded Maui's rule further than any other mō'ī. He reigned when Captain James Cook arrived in the islands (1778) and he died at Waikiki in 1794. Kalanikūpule, his son, was the last in line of the Maui chiefs, for due to infighting with his uncle, Kaeokulani, Maui

This is a reconstructed koʻa or fish shrine at the Maui Ocean Center Aquarium beside Māʻalaea Harbor in the Wailuku district, Maui.

was weakened and Hawaiʻi Island chief, Kamehameha the Great, swept across Maui on his way to establish the Kingdom of Hawaiʻi with all of the islands united.

In 1786, French admiral Jean-François de La Perouse was the first western explorer to actually land on Maui. Many traders, whalers, loggers and eventually missionaries (1823) followed.

With Kamehameha's death the old religion passed into history as the aliʻi dismantled the kapu system and destroyed the heiau, even before the first Christian missionaries arrived. King Kamehameha II, III, IV, and V would see the seat of government slowly shift with the changing centers of commerce, moving from the Big Island of Hawaiʻi to Lahaina, Maui, with the whaling and sandalwood trade, then on to Honolulu on Oʻahu with the sugar industry. Due to shifts in power, the changes in commerce, and because of western diseases the population of Maui decreased over the nineteenth and early twentieth centuries. The Great Mehele of 1848 divided up the lands and ushered in the buying and selling of property rights and the establishment of land ownership. Sugarcane and ranching sustained Maui through most of this time and into the mid-twentieth century. Captain George Vancouver, who sailed as a junior officer with Cook, returned to the islands in 1793 with a gift of cattle for Kamehameha I that were let loose and declared kapu. Eventually the small herd multiplied to such an extent that ranches had to be established to manage what had become a major ecological problem. Paniolo (cowboys) were brought in from Mexico to train Hawaiians in the art of cow punching, today a way of life for many in the upcountry and backside areas of the island. Apparently, Vancouver also gave permission to the young Hawaiian Kingdom to use the British union jack as part of the Hawaiian flag.

Today, tourism and the military are Hawai'i's mainstay industry. Close to three million tourists visit Maui each year. As a result the island population has grown again to over 150,000 residents. The statewide population is 1.4 million. With the growth in population, development, and preservation come into active confrontation. Since it's early settlement, Maui, has been the site of great power struggles and conflicts. Between Hawai'i Island to the southeast and the leeward islands to the northwest, Maui's very shape suggests this tension of being pulled in opposite directions. Because of constant exchange, not just through conflict and warfare in the past, Maui has served as a kind of cultural funnel for the island chain. In many ways Maui is two different islands with the central valley isthmus acting as a third mediating region. It was here

This reproduction of a petroglyph of a double-hulled sailing canoe is from a cliff face at Kalialinui Gulch in the Makawao district, Maui.

that the high chiefs settled and it is here that present-day local government and commerce have made their home. Most visitors today will arrive on Maui in this area, at the Kahului Airport (OGG) or the harbor.

Before visiting the ancient sites of Maui you might stop in at the Bailey House Museum with its collection of late Hawaiian and early post-contact artifacts (see Appendix B). The Maui Historical Society and Archive is also located at the museum. Open Monday through Friday, 10 AM to 4 PM, the museum is located at 2375-A Main Street, Wailuku 96793. Phone: 244-3326. On the far eastern end of the island Hāna Cultural Center and Museum hosts a small collection of Hawaiian artifacts and is open Monday through Saturday, 11 AM to 4 PM, located at Uakea Road near Hāna Bay. Phone: 248-8622. (1; 2; 3; 5; 7; 8; 10; 11; 14; 15; 20; 21; 22; 23; 27; 30; 35; 36; 37; 39; 40; 42)

'O Maui nō ka 'oi.
Maui is the best.

—Hawaiian saying

MAUI SITE MAP

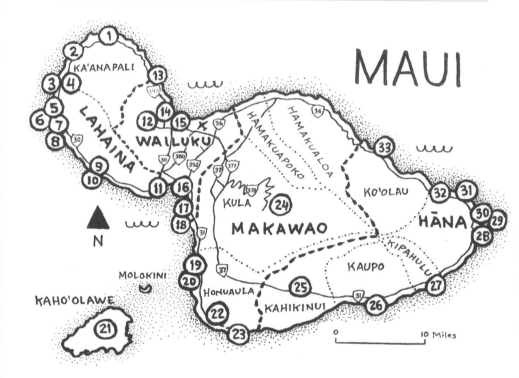

MAUI

KA'ANAPALI
LAHAINA
WAILUKU
HAMAKUAPOKO
HAMAKUALOA
KO'OLAU
HĀNA
KULA
MAKAWAO
KIPAHULU
KAUPO
HONUAULA
KAHIKINUI
MOLOKINI
KAHO'OLAWE

N

0   10 Miles

Maui Site List

I. **Lahaina (West Maui)**

1. Kahakuloa
2. Kapalua
3. Puʻu Kekaʻa (Black Rock)
4. Pōhaku Moemoe and Wahine Peʻe
5. Pōhaku Hauola
6. Lahaina
7. Mokuʻula and Loko Mokuhinia
8. Hale Piula
9. Olowalu Petroglyphs
10. Olowalu Landing

II. **Wailuku (Central Maui)**

11. Pōhaku O Māʻalaea
12. Īao Valley (State Park)
13. Waiheʻe Coastal Dune and Wetlands Refuge
14. Halekiʻi and Pihanakalani Heiau
15. Kanahā Pond (State Wildlife Sanctuary)
16. Keālia Pond (National Wildlife Refuge)
17. Kōʻieʻie Fishpond
18. Koʻa i Kamaʻole

III. **Makawao (South Maui and Upcountry)**

19. Wailea
20. Palauea Cultural Preserve
21. Kahoʻolawe
22. Keoneʻōʻio (La Perouse Archaeological District)
23. Hoapili Trail
24. Haleakalā (National Park)

IV. **Hāna (East Maui)**

25. Kahikinui
26. Nuʻu Landing and Kaupo
27. ʻOheʻo and Kīpahulu
28. Haneoʻo and Kuamaka Fishponds
29. Ka Iwi O Pele
30. Kaʻuiki Head
31. Waiʻānapanapa (State Park)
32. Piʻilanihale Heiau
33. Keʻanae

MAUI SITE LOCATIONS

I. West Maui: Lahaina

The area known as Lahaina encompasses all of West Maui, including the western slopes of the West Maui Mountains and the Kā'anapali district. The old pronunciation, Lāhainā, means "cruel sun," and was apparently given to this leeward region because of regular droughts. It is told that Hua, a chief of Lahaina, killed his kahuna and, for this reason, the curse of a terrible drought came upon the land. However, just above the coastal areas of residential and resort development, the Lahaina land section supports substantial crop cultivation which is well irrigated from the regular rains in the mountains. Lele is the ancient name for this area, which means "altar" and "flight," and it is referred to in chants as a place supporting orchards of breadfruit trees. Another old name for Lahaina was Honoapi'ilani, meaning the "bays of Chief Pi'ilani," from which one can see the islands of Moloka'i, Lāna'i, and Kaho'olawe, all ruled by the ancient ali'i Pi'ilani.

Many important battles took place in this area. One, in the early 18th century, involved two half-brothers struggling for control of West Maui. On his deathbed, chief Kekaulike named his youngest son, Kamehamehanui, as his heir. Normally the eldest son would have become high chief, but because the mother of Kamehamehanui was sister to Alapa'inui, the Hawai'i Island chief, Kekaulike correctly assumed that Alapa'inui would not attack his nephew in order to conquer Maui. Kauhi, the elder half-brother, was so enraged over his disinheritance that he went to war against his younger brother with an army of 600 warriors he had enlisted from O'ahu. Alapa'inui came to his nephew Kamehamehanui's aid with 8,000 warriors, and for four days a battle raged from the village of Lahaina along the coast into Kā'anapali. Finally, with many slain on both sides, Kauhi and the O'ahu forces were overcome. Because losses on both sides were so great, the battle became known as Koko o nā Moku ("Blood of the Islands").

Nearly 100 years later, following his conquest of Maui, Kamehameha the Great of Hawai'i Island headquartered his war fleet at Lahaina and planned for the invasions of Moloka'i, Lāna'i, and O'ahu. In 1820, Kamehameha III drew up the first Hawaiian constitution here, and established Lahaina as the capital of the Islands, which it remained until 1845. Moku'ula and Loko Mokuhinia Lahaina were the royal center of the Hawaiian Kingdom and the port town thus became an active gathering place for whalers and missionaries in those early days. In addition to its ancient sites, Lahaina has many early post-contact sites that you can locate with the help of self-guiding maps found at numerous shops and tourist information locations in Lahaina town.

There were numerous heiau, places of ritual practice, in this area but few of them remain today and those that do are not accessible to the public. Some of the temple names that are remembered in the Lahaina District are: Kahana Heiau, Mailepai Heiau, Hihiho Heiau, Kahauiki Heiau, Honuaula Heiau, Ililike Heiau, Kāneola Heiau, Kuewa Heiau, Keahialoa Heiau, Pakao Heiau, Waipiliamo'o Heiau, and Kukuipuka Heiau.

A few hotels in West Maui display ancient artifacts excavated from their sites. The Ritz-Carlton at Kapalua shares its West Maui site with

Pu'eone 'O Honokahua burial grounds is a sacred Hawaiian site dating back to at least AD 850. It may only be viewed from a distance.

Olowalu Petroglyphs are an important example of ancient Hawaiian carved story-pictures, ki'i pōhaku.

the Pu'eone 'O Honokahua burial grounds, where thousands of ancient Hawaiian remains dating from AD 850, are laid to rest. This is an especially sacred site and may only be viewed from a distance.

There are a number of storied-stones in this part of Maui with fascinating tales connected to them. From the bellstone Pōhaku O Kani, to Pu'u Keka'a, Pōhaku Moemoe, Pōhaku Wahine Pe'e, and in Lahaina town, the healing stone Pōhaku Hauola, the sacred stones all tell of ancient sagas. The picture-stones or petroglyphs of Olowalu are also of special importance for this area. Lahaina was clearly an important region in the Hawaiian Islands and an important wahi pana of Maui. (2; 4; 20; 32; 37)

> *Hālau Lahaina, malu i ka 'ulu.*
> *Lahaina is like a large house in the shade of breadfruit trees.*
>
> —Hawaiian saying

West Maui: Lahaina District Map

KAPALUA

KAHAKULOA

N

②

①

KĀ'ANAPALI

340

PU'U
KEKA'A

③

PŌHAKU
MOEMOE
AND
WAHINE
PE'E

④

PŌHAKU
HAUOLA

⑤

⑥ LAHAINA

WAILUKU
DISTRICT

MOKU'ULA
AND
LOKO
MOKUHINIA

⑦

⑧

HALE PIULA

OLOWALU LANDING

⑨

⑩

OLOWALU
PETROGLYPHS

30

LAHAINA
DISTRICT

I.I **Kahakuloa**

Coastal land area

Kahakuloa ("the tall lord" or "far away master") is a small village on the north shore of West Maui, on a bay and in an ahupua'a (small land division) of the same name. The larger land area is called Ka'anapali ("division cliff"), which is the pie-shaped northern part of the still larger Lahaina District. Although present day Ka'anapali is only considered the smaller resort area just north of Lahaina town and south of the Kapalua West Maui Airport, the ancient designation of Ka'anapali was of this much larger area that stretches from Keka'a Point (see site I.3 Pu'u Keka'a) along the coast north and then east to Makamaka'ole and up to 5788-foot Pu'u Kukui, the highest point in the West Maui Mountains and one of the wettest spots on earth receiving over 400 inches of rain annually.

Along the coastal highway of this land section to the north, just outside the village of Kahakuloa, is the bellstone known as Pōhaku O

Kani. On the mauka side of the road, this "sounding" stone, like many others found throughout the Islands, was "rung" at special times by striking it with a large stick. The stone is also said to have been a place for hiding the umbilical cord stumps of newborns in order to bring the children mana or spiritual strength. Unfortunately, there are no known legends connected with this stone. Please don't strike the stone!

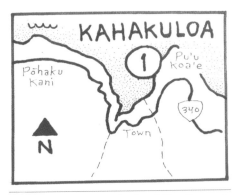

Tradition tells of Pōhaku o Kane (not to be confused with the bellstone Pōhaku o Kani mentioned above), a large rock 7-feet long and 6-feet tall, on the

LOCATION: **Kahakuloa is about 22 miles north of Lahaina town along Honoapiʻilani Hwy., and the bellstone Pōhaku O Kani is just before one enters the town on the right side of the highway, not far past the second 41-mile marker. Coming from Kahakuloa, Pōhaku O Kani is just past the 16-mile marker.**

east side of the valley slope, north of the church. It was apparently a place of ritual practice in former times. There was also a petroglyph rock found at Kahakuloa that had human figures etched into it in the linear body type. Two unusual male figures were rendered with disjointed bodies. The stone was taken into Kahului and is no longer at Kahakuloa.

Pōhaku O Kani is an example of a Hawaiian bellstone. Like many others found throughout the Islands it was "rung" at special times by striking it with a large stick.

Pu'u Koae ("tropicbird hill"), the 636-foot headland jutting out into the bay, is also called Elephant Rock by locals and has a ledge known as Kahekili's Leap.

There was also a pu'uhonua or place of refuge here that served all of West Maui. Such places could mean salvation from the death penalty for kapu breakers. Some heiau in and around Kahakuloa were Kane-ola, Kuewa, Keahialoa, Pakao, and Waipiliamo'o Heiau. There was an ancient ko'a or fishing shrine on the beach but it is now destroyed as are the heiau.

The steep 636-foot promantory above the bay, Pu'u Koae ("tropicbird hill"), was said in one tale to be the home of Kahekili, and upon rising each day he would leap into the ocean below for his refreshing morning swim. He would then scale the cliff face to get back up for his breakfast. The spot is known as Kahekili's Leap. The site was also used as a look-out and a story is told that during the wars with Kalaniopu'u of Hawai'i a sentinel was posted here on a ledge where there was an outcrop of stone 2-feet thick. The guard apparently made an insulting gesture as Kalaniopu'u's canoes approached Pu'u Koae and Kalaniopu'u unexpect-edly threw a stone the amazingly great distance up at guard. It is said that the stone broke a hole right through the ledge outcrop striking and killing the offending sentinel who plunged to his death in the sea below. A 15-inch hole is left in the rock ledge and the Bishop Museum is re-ported as having in its collection a 2-pound stone that is said to be the lethal object that was thrown by the warrior chief (item #4047 on page 76 of the *Preliminary Catalog*, Part II).

Pu'u Koae is called Elephant Rock by locals as one can well see from across the bay. The ledge of Kahekili's Leap can also be seen from this vantage point on the bay's westside. (4; 10; 32; 37; 40)

1.2 **Kapalua**

Coastal land area

In ancient times those living in upper Kapalua ("two borders" or "arms embracing the sea") grew kalo (taro) and the bay was a productive fishing ground. In 1836, Dwight Baldwin, a missionary doctor arrived on Maui and was eventually awarded a royal land grant of 2,675 acreas for farming and grazing. By 1902, the Honolua Ranch as it was called then, had grown to 24,000 acres. Cultivating pineapples, the family ranch became

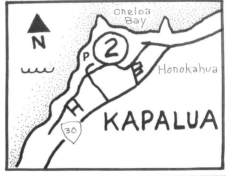

LOCATION: **Kapalua is about 8.1 miles north of Lahaina town along Honoapi'ilani Hwy.**

Baldwin Packers, the largest private label pineapple company. In 1946, Baldwin Packers merged with Maui Land & Pineapple Company. Led by a 5th generation descendent of the Baldwin family the Kapalua Resort was created on some of the company land in the 1980s.

In 1986 the Maui Planning Commission approved a permit for Kapalua Land Company to develop a hotel on the sand dunes overlooking Honokahua Bay. It was known that archaeological sites and Hawaiian burials were in the sand. There were no laws protecting burial sites at the time but by 1987 the Hawaiian group Hui Alanui O Makena, togetherer with the Office of Hawaiian Affairs, worked out an arrangement with the developer, following prolonged protests, for a respectful excavation process. The number of remains was not known at that time. By 1988, 800 human remains had been excavated with no end in sight. In December of that year Governor John Waihe'e (a Native Hawaiian) called a halt to the excavation and initiated a new agreement. It was decided to move the hotel 500 yards uphill from the site and the state would pay $5.5 million to create a preservation easement and another $500,000 for restoring the excavation site. More than 2,000 remains were eventually excavated and reinterred at Kapalua. Archaeologists determined that some of the remains dated back to the 9th century AD Artifacts with some of the burials indicated a number of high-ranking ali'i were among those layed to rest. The site also included a portion of the 16th century Alaloa or Pi'ilani Trail, a paved footpath that once circled the island. Kahauiki Heiau was also reported to be in this area but now destroyed.

Many reforms, in particular the establishment of the island Burial Council, came about as a result of the protests surrounding the Kapalua development. A song by Hawaiian activist Charles Kauluwehi Maxwell, Sr. celebrated the preservation victory with the concluding verse:

> *Ha'ina 'ia mai ana ka puana*
> *E Honokahua 'āina nani maoli*
> *Na Hono kaulana a o Pi'ilani*
> *'Ia wahi kapu nā kupuna e*
> *'Ia wahi kapu nā kupuna e*
> *'Ia wahi kapu nā kupuna e*

> Tell the story, give praise to
> The beautiful land of Honokahua
> With its famous bay of Pi'ilani
> It shall not be disturbed, this place where our ancestors sleep
> It shall not be disturbed, this place where our ancestors sleep
> It shall not be disturbed, this place where our ancestors sleep

Today the Ritz-Carlton at Kapalua luxury resort and golf course shares its site with the 13.6-acre Pu'eone 'O Honokahua burial ground, a sacred Hawaiian wahi pana dating back to c. AD 850. Reserved exclusively for Native Hawaiian religious and ceremonial practices the site is enclosed by a hedge with commemorative markers. Remain on the marked pathways and please respect the sacred burial place. Public entry is prohibited but one can view the site from a respectable distance. The Ritz-Carlton at Kapalua has a Hawaiian Cultural Advisor, Clifford Nae'ole, who conducts weekly "Sense of Place" discussions and tours to the border of the preserve. For information on cultural activities contact the hotel at 808-669-6200 or www.ritzcarlton.com/ kapalua. (2; 4; 10; 32; 37; 40)

Pu'eone 'O Honokahua, a sacred Hawaiian burial ground dating to c.AD 850, is Reserved exclusively for Native Hawaiian religious and ceremonial practices, and is marked by commemorative plaques and sculpture, and enclosed with a hedge.

1.3 **Pu'u Keka'a (Black Rock)**

Coastal lava rock cliff

Pu'u Keka'a ("hill of the rumble" [as in thunder]), known today as Black Rock, is the most prominent natural feature at Kā'anapali. Formed by an old lava flow that entered the sea, this work of the volcano goddess Pele creates a little cove, with beaches on either side that attract abundant marine life. It was very sacred to ancient Hawaiians as a leina a ka 'uhane ("leaping off spot of the spirit" or "leap of the soul"), where souls depart or leap over into the spirit world at death. Pu'u Keka'a also means the "turning point hill," and was a marker for the division between Lahaina and Ka'anapali.

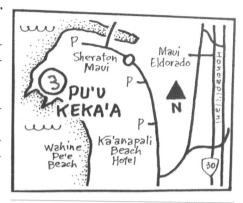

LOCATION: **At the northern end of Wahine Pe'e Beach, behind the Sheraton-Maui Resort. Approached from the public beach access beside the Kā'anapali Beach Hotel.**

Māui the demi-god is said to have begun many of his legendary exploits from this neighborhood, and later battles were fought here because of the close proximity to the departing place for the dead that was considered advantageous to the warriors who would lose their lives while fighting. A heiau was situated on top of the sacred pu'u (hill), where the Sheraton-Maui Resort now stands, and Keka'a, an old farming and fishing village, was located near the beach between the Royal Lahaina Hotel and the Maui Eldorado Condominiums.

Keka'a was the birthplace of Kaululā'au, the wayward son of Kaka'alāneo, who was exiled to Lāna'i for cutting down an orchard of breadfruit trees. On Lāna'i he fought and overcame all the ghosts that made that island uninhabitable and, for this deed, was welcomed home a hero.

Kahekili, known as "the thunderer," was the last great Maui chief. He ruled the island for 27 years, beginning in 1766, and, through warfare and marriage, expanded his domain to include all the Hawaiian Islands except Kaua'i and Hawai'i. Three times during his reign Kahekili threw off invasions of Maui instigated by Big Island chief, Kalani'ōpu'u. Later Kahekili's armies fought in decisive battles against Kamehameha the Great. Once, when Kamehameha sent a messenger to Kahekili to negotiate whether or not they should have another war, Kahekili sent back a reply to the young Hawai'i chief to wait until the aged Maui chief was dead and burial rites were performed before coming against Maui in war again. This is just what Kamehameha did.

In his prime, Kahekili was honored for his ability as an athlete of lele kawa (to leap feet first from high sea cliffs into the ocean). There are places on O'ahu and Lāna'i known as Kahekili's Leap. However, Pu'u Keka'a is where the Maui chief made his most impressive jumps. Only someone with tremendous mana could jump and return unharmed

The Sheraton Maui Resort often features cliff jumping at sunset, easily viewed from its beach on the south side of Black Rock or Puʻu Kekaʻa. According to tradition, High Chief Kahekili did this leap from here many times.

from where the souls of the dead leapt over into the other world. According to tradition, Kahekili did this many times at Puʻu Kekaʻa.

The Sheraton Maui Resort often features cliff jumping at sunset, easily viewed from the beach on the south side of Puʻu Kekaʻa. (2/6, 4; 10; 14; 32/64; 37/47-48; 40)

I.4 **Pōhaku Moemoe and Pōhaku Wahine Peʻe**

Two boulders

Moemoe was a legendary companion of the demigod Māui. Just as Māui was always active, creating and doing things, Moemoe was always tired, sleepy, and lazying about. Moemoe was called the "Sleeper of Kekaʻa" because he lived at Kekaʻa village, in Kāʻanapali, and was always napping at just about any time. His name is still used in Hawaiian when referring to a sleepy person.

One day Māui was setting off to slow down the course of the sun so that his mother could have more time to beat her kapa cloth, when Moemoe recommended that Māui relax and rest

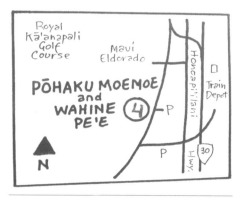

LOCATION: **Take Kekaʻa Drive makai (toward the sea) off Honoapiʻilani Hwy. to south end of the Maui Eldorado Condominiums. The stones are in amongst shrubbery at the edge of the Royal Kaʻanapali North Golf Course.**

himself before taking on such a task or he would surely not succeed. However, Māui would not hear of it and promptly pursued his destiny.

Upon his triumphant return to Keka'a, Māui turned Moemoe into stone for being so lazy and doubting Māui's ability to alter the path of the sun. To this day the sun shines longer in the summer because of Maui's deed and his companion sleeps soundly as Pōhaku Moemoe.

Beside Pōhaku Moemoe is another stone called Pōhaku Wahine Pe'e. The "hiding woman," Wahine Pe'e, was a guardian spirit who dwelt in the body of a pueo (owl). She lived with other spirits in a cave called Ke Ana Pueo ("the Owl Cave"), which was located where the third and fourth holes of the Royal Kā'anapali North Golf Course are now.

Once, a young boy named Kā'ili was kidnapped from the beach near Keka'a by warriors in need of a human sacrifice. The boy was to be offered to the war god at Haluluko'ako'a Heiau, a large luakini (human sacrifice) temple near Lahaina. Nā'ilima, the boy's sister, saw Kā'ili taken by the men and fled to the mouth of Ke Ana Pueo, where she be-

Upon his triumphant return capturing the sun, Māui turned Moemoe into stone for being so lazy and doubting Māui's ability to alter the path of the sun. To this day Pōhaku Moemoe sleeps soundly at Keka'a. Beside Pōhaku Moemoe is another stone, Pōhaku Wahine Pe'e which looks like an owl's head.

gan to cry. Responding to the situation, the owl-spirit, Wahine Pe'e, flew to the temple's sacrificial stone, where Kā'ili had been tied-up to wait until the next morning's ritual service. Wahine Pe'e freed the boy and instructed him to walk backwards out of the sacred precinct and along the beach to where he had been captured by the warriors. Kā'ili carefully made his backward footprints in the sand, leaving no impression of anyone having left the heiau. Wahine Pe'e took both the children to a cave atop Pu'u Keka'a, where they waited while the confused warriors searched for their missing sacrifice. When the search was abandoned, Kā'ili and Nā'ilima returned safely to their village.

Wahine Pe'e is also known as Pōhaku o Wahine o Manua and is associated with the story of a woman who ran away from her abusive husband. She hid at Haluluko'ako'a Heiau, even though the coral temple was kapu to women. An owl god appeared and led her to a rock near Keka'a, where she slept until morning. At dawn she awoke and departed from the Lahaina district, never to return to her husband.

The spirit of Wahine Pe'e eventually came to rest in a stone that looks like the head of an owl and, together with Pōhaku Moemoe, now lies amidst shrubbery on the grounds of the Maui Eldorado Condominiums. (2/8; 32/106; 37/48-50; 40)

I.5 **Pōhaku Hauola**

Boulder in shallow water

Hauola ("dew of life") is a large boulder, shaped somewhat like a couch, lying in shallow water at Lahaina town. It is said to have been a woman fleeing from enemies whom the gods saved by turning to stone. Hauola is also the name of an ancient surfing area at Lahaina.

According to tradition, Pōhaku Hauola contains supernatural forces used for healing. Kāhuna helped to ease and cure their patients' ills by having them lie across healing stones such as Pōhaku Hauola. For instance, labor pains were said to be relieved by sitting on certain water-washed stones. In addition to herbal remedies, special diets, and lomilomi (massage) therapy, healing stones were an important component

According to tradition, Pōhaku Hauola contains supernatural forces used for heal-ing. Kāhuna helped to ease and cure their patients' ills by having them lie upon this healing stone in shallow water. It was also used as a birthing stone and place to leave umbilical cord stumps.

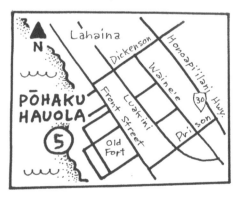

LOCATION: **Take Kekaʻa Drive makai (to-ward the sea) off Honoapiʻilani Hwy. to south end of the Maui Eldorado Con-dominiums. The stones are in amongst shrubbery at the edge of the Royal Kaʻanapali North Golf Course.**

in ancient Hawaiian medical practice. Hauola was also used as a birthing stone where labor pains would be diminished and easy passage into the world of the living was said to take place. Another ancient practice connected with such stones was the placing of umbilical cord stumps of newborn children in the holes and crevices in order to draw mana into them and empower the newborn. Such stones as Hauola are found on all of the Hawaiian Islands, but most have long since been forgotten.

Pōhaku Hauola can be seen at the water's edge just below the coastal retaining wall. The site is marked by an informational sign. (32/42; 37/34; 40)

> *Ka Laʻi o Hauola.*
> The calm of Hauola.
> [Peace and comfort. There is a stone in the sea at Lahaina, Maui, called Pōhaku o Hauola, where pregnant women went to sit to ensure an easy birth. The umbilical cords of babies were hidden in crevices in the stone.] (31/154)
> —Hawaiian saying

I.6 Lahaina

Former capital of the Hawaiian Kingdom

Lele was the ancient name for Lahaina, and Lā hainā means "cruel sun" referring to this hot and dry leeward area of the island. Lahaina receives about 13 inches of rain a year compared to over 400 inches at Puʻu Kukui, the highest summit in the West Maui Mountains.

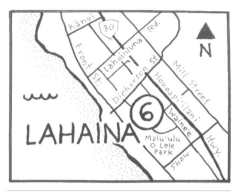

LOCATION: **About 22 miles from Kahului via Honoapiʻilani Hwy.**

In 1795, Kamehameha the Great sacked Lahaina as he conquered Maui and went on to unite the other Hawaiian Islands. Lahaina was later the capital of the Kingdom of Hawaiʻi from 1820 to 1845 under the reign of Kamehameha III, son of Kamehameha the Great. At this time Lahaina was the global center of the whaling industry. Tensions between the newly arrived Christian missionaries trying to "civilize" the natives and the routie whalers try-

In 1832 Lahaina Fort was built in response to the shelling by an English whaler of missionary premises. A corner of the coral block wall ruins can still be seen.

ing to gain advantage of them often ran high. More than once whalers opened fire on Lahaina in protest of the missionaries devout and restrictive ways. In 1824 the first mission school west of the Mississippi, Lahainluna, was opened here.

A few paces from Pōhaku Hauola (site I.4) at the waterfront in Lahaina town, is the former site of Kamehameha the Great's Brick Palace. Built sometime between 1798 and 1802 for Queen Ka'ahumanu, the Brick Palace was the first western style building in the islands and was used during the early 1800s to welcome the captains of visiting ships. However, the queen preferred a traditional thatched hale. Many international trade deals would have been sealed in this humble structure. Sandwood was the major trade item used by chiefs to gain western goods. The Western-style structure was brick on the outside but paneled entirely with wood on the inside. It measured 40 by 20 feet, was two stories tall, and had four rooms with glazed windows. The Brick Palace was used for more than 60 years as a meeting house and later as a storehouse, but the brickwork began to sag after 10 years and plaster could only preserve it until the 1860s. All that remains at the site is a restored brick foundation plan.

In the center of town, along Front Street in Banyan Tree Square, is the former site of Lahaina Fort. Maui governor Hoapili ordered construction of the fort in 1827 in response to the shelling of the missionary compound by an English whaler. It was built in 1832 over an original mud and sand fort in the same location. A corner of the coral block wall ruins can still be seen. Coral was cut from the reef about 40 yards off shore and salvaged canons from ships sunk in Hawaiian waters were mounted on the walls. Some 47 guns of varying sizes were rarely fired except to commemorate Kamehameha III's birthday. Such coral structures were built in early post-contact Hawai'i before it was realized how destructive the removal of coral was to the living reef system around the islands. The former prison, on Prison Street, is another such construction. In 1854 when the fort was demolished the coral blocks were carried off and used in other construction projects elsewhere in town.

Banyan Tree Square is named for the now extensive banyan tree that was planted here in 1873 by William Owen Smith in commemoration of the 50th anniversary of the arrival of the missionaries. The single tree has grown and spread and been trimmed back to provide a pleasant shaded square. There are numerous other early historic buildings in the area, mostly of the missionary, monarchy, and territorial periods. (15; 22; 32; 37; 40)

1.7 **Mokuʻula and Loko Mokuhinia**

Former island and fishpond

The sacred island of Mokuʻula was located in the royal fishpond of Mokuhinia at Lahaina. The island was about one acre in size, and the fishpond surrounding it was between 11 and 17 acres, with numerous smaller, sister ponds in the immediate vicinity. Mokuʻula was abandoned in the middle of the last century, when the fishpond began to dry up, and, in 1972, the last remaining pond was filled. The site has been converted into a county recreational area, known as Malu ʻulu o Lele ("breadfruit shelter of Lele") Park and none of the ancient features remain today. However, that may change.

It was in Lahaina that the famous Maui chief Piʻilani died. It was here, also, that Kihaapiʻilani, son of Piʻilani, had a daughter, Kihawahine. When Kihawahine died, she was deified as the moʻo (lizard-like water being) of Mokuhinia fishpond. Under her protection, the pond and

Moku'ula island remained kapu and sacred to high-ranking ali'i, especially those of the lineage of Pi'ilani. When Kamehameha I conquered Maui he cleverly married into the Pi'ilani line. As king of the Hawaiian Islands, Kamehameha and the sons who succeeded him used Moku'ula as their royal residence in Lahaina, and showed honor to Kihawahine. The revered mo'o was said to live beneath Moku'ula in an underwater cave called Kalua o Kiha ("den of Kiha").

Lahaina was the capital of the Hawaiian Kingdom from 1820

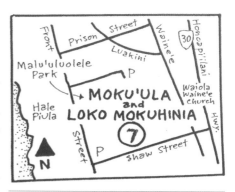

LOCATION: **Eastend of Lahaina town center, along Front Street, between Mokuhina and Shaw Streets, in Malu'ulu o Lele Park. There is parking at the corner of Front and Shaw Streets.**

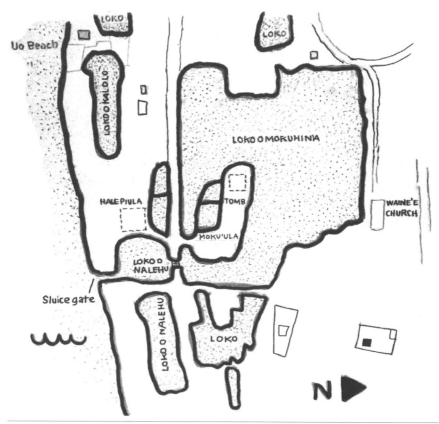

The above map approximates how this part of Lahaina, the kapu island of Moku'ula and the royal fishpond of Mokuhinia, looked in 1848.

Waineʻe Cemetery, just behind the Malu ʻulu o Lele Park, is the burial ground of some of the early Hawaiian royalty. Kapu Queen Keōpūolani, wife of Kamehameha I and mother of Kamehameha III, and High Chief Kaumualiʻi, the last king of Kauaʻi are among those aliʻi layed to rest here. Kaumualiʻi requested to be buried near Keōpūolani.

until 1845 and prominently displayed the extremes that the western world had imported to the Islands by way of whalers, merchants, and missionaries. King Kalani Kauikeaouli, Kamehameha III, spent much of his time at Mokuʻula. He was a recluse, a drinker, and not at all sympathetic to Christianity in contrast to many of his regents and advisors. He wanted to see a return to the ways of old Hawaiʻi, but the times were changing rapidly. He sought to ensure that his lineage would be of the highest aliʻi blood by taking his sister as his wife, but she and their three infant children all met with early deaths. The grieving king placed his sister, Nāhiʻenaʻena, and their children together with his deceased mother Queen Keōpūolani, in a royal mausoleum on the island of Mokuʻula. The remains of each royal family member were placed in a coffin of zinc, within a second coffin of lead, surrounded by an outer, wooden coffin. Beside the mausoleum, in a small native-style "palace," the king lived near his departed loved ones. Because of the kapu on Loko Mokuhinia, Kamehameha III's privacy was respected. In 1837, after giving up drinking, Kamehameha III married Kalama, the daughter of a minor Kona chief. They lived at Lahaina until the government moved to Honolulu in 1845. The king died in 1854.

Little is known about Mokuʻula immediately following the death of the king. It is said that Bernice Pauahi Bishop came to the island in 1883 and, with a following of aliʻi, removed the remains from the old royal mausoleum on the island and relocated them to their present resting place at Waineʻe Cemetery, just behind the park. Other Hawaiian royalty buried at Waineʻe were High Chief Kaumualiʻi, the last king of Kauaʻi; High Chief Hoapili, a general and close friend of Kamehameha I; High Chiefess Liliha, granddaughter of Kahekili, last king of Maui (she led a rebellion on Oʻahu in 1830, when she was governor there); and Kalakua Hoapili Wahine, one of Kamehameha's queens and governor of Maui from 1840 to 1842, who helped start Lahainaluna, the first Christian school west of the Rocky Mountains. The oldest Christian gravestone in Hawaiʻi is at this cemetery. Dated 1829, it was for a local Maui native who died of "fever."

Mokuʻula was abandoned and Loko Mokuhinia was neglected until the island was leveled and the pond filled in 1918. The last of the royal ponds in this area was filled with dirt and coral in the early 1970s. In 1993, the Bishop Museum undertook a preliminary excavation of the Mokuʻula site, which rallied tremendous community support and involvement. Over 200 volunteers participated in the dig, unearthing glass and pottery fragments, bones of fish, cows, pigs, and, most of all, dogs. (Dog was the preferred offering to Kihawahine, the guardian moʻo of Mokuhinia fishpond.) Stonewalls, post holes, and possible foundation rocks of the royal mausoleum were located, and well-preserved wooden planks that may have been part of a landing dock for Mokuʻula were discovered.

Maui County and the people of Lahaina are presently considering their options for the future, which include moving the park and restoring a part of the archaeological site at Mokuʻula within a park setting or restoring the sacred isle and the royal fishpond in its entirety. Though Mokuʻula and Loko Mokuhinia are not visible sites at present, they are certainly not forgotten. (Ka ʻElele, March-April ʻ93/2; 15; 22; 32; 37/39; 40)

> *E hoʻi ka nani i Mokuʻula.*
> Let the glory return to Mokuʻula.
> —19th century chant by P.H. Kekuaiwa

I.8 **Hale Piula**

House site foundation

Makai (toward the ocean) of Malu 'ulu o Lele Park, Moku'ula and Loko Mokuhinia (site I.7), across Front Street, is the site of Hale Piula ("the iron roof house"), a palace built for Kamehameha III in the 1830s. He did not care for the Western structure and preferred to sleep in a typical Hawaiian thatched hale, so the palace was never completed. Following the Great Mahele in 1848, when land could be bought and sold, this area remained crown property. In 1858, Hale Piula was damaged by a storm, and most of its stones were carried away and used to

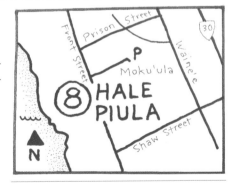

LOCATION: **At the eastern end of Lahaina town center, along Front Street, between Mokuhina and Shaw Streets, across from Malu'ulu o Lele Park. There is parking at the corner of Front and Shaw Streets.**

Hale Piula was surrounded on all sides by water; the ocean, fishponds, and canals. Puna or springs flowed down from Kaua'ula Valley in the West Maui Mountains via underground lava tubes feeding Loko Mokuhinia and flowing through the canals to the sea.

build a new courthouse on Wharf Street. The hale (house) foundation now has a wood and thatch structure with open sides much like a traditional Hawaiian building.

Hale Piula was surrounded by water on all sides; ocean, fishponds, and canals. Puna or springs flowed down from Kaua'ula Valley in the West Maui Mountains via underground lava tubes feeding the fishponds. The fishponds were plentiful and the fresh water flowed out to the ocean through a mākāhā or sluice gate, just south of the hale. Wai ("water") was a symbol of wealth (waiwai means "weath") and was essential to the royal power. This ahupua'a (land division) is called Waine'e ("flowing water").

Just off shore was called Ka Papa Limu a Pi'ilani ("the seaweed reef of Pi'ilani") because of the great variety of reef seaweed available in these waters. Thrownet fishing and surfing were also popular here.

An ahu (altar) stands in front of the hale and informational signs describe the history and significance of the area. (37; 40)

1.9 **Olowalu Petroglyphs**

Rock engravings

The petroglyphs at Olowalu ("many hills") are situated along a basalt cliff face on the west side of a promontory called Kīlea ("small but conspicuous hill") within the former sugar cane fields of West Maui. Twelve hills here are said to be associated with the twelve months of the lunar year, with Kīlea being the thirteenth. A dirt road runs directly parallel to Olowalu Gulch and winds towards the tall green mountains to the north that create the spectacular Olowalu Canyon, in the ahupua'a of Lihau. Well before the canyon, a rock outcropping on

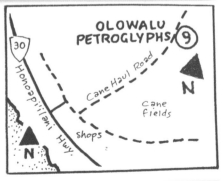

LOCATION: **Six-tenths of a mile heading mauka (towards the mountains) behind the Olowalu General Store, off Honoapi'ilani Highway, route 30. Turn at the old water tower and follow the telephone poles on an unpaved road to the rock outcrop with petroglyphs on the right.**

A rock outcropping on the right reveals a gallery of ki'i pōhaku, petroglyphs, etched on the rockface. The petroglyph site is cared for by the non-profit group Olowalu Cultural Reserve.

More than 100 engraved images, including human figures, animals, and "crab-claw" sails, can be seen at Olowalu Cultural Reserve (see page 48).

the right reveals a gallery of ki'i pōhaku, petroglyphs or etched rock art.

It is here that some 100 finely engraved images, including human figures, animals, and "crab-claw" sails, can be seen. It is thought that some of the carvings may indicate journeys, events, or significant legends. They may also be gestures to ensure long life and personal health. Petroglyphs are often found at ancient boundaries.

In 1964, the Lahaina Restoration Foundation acquired a lease to the site, as well as a public right-of-way, and built a wooden stairway and viewing stand for visitors to observe the ancient art. However, the site has since suffered from neglect and the stairs have been removed. Viewing of the petroglyphs should be done from the road below. Now, the petroglyph site is cared for by the non-profit group Olowalu Cultural Reserve (214-8778).

Not far from Olowalu Petroglyphs is the well-preserved Ka'iwaloa Heiau. However, permission is required to visit the heiau. Contact the Pioneer Mill Company in Lahaina for information on the accessibility of the heiau.

Unfortunately, in recent years graffiti and vandelism have marred the Olowalu Petroglyph site. Please remember not to touch, draw on or around, deface or damage the petroglyphs in any way. These are very rare and precious documents of ancient Hawai'i. Please protect them. (4/55; 6/11, 92-93; 21/64; 24/17; 37/25; 40)

I.10 **Olowalu Landing**

Ancient canoe landing

In 1790, Olowalu was the site of a cruel and bloody massacre when Captain Simon Metcalf of the American ship Eleanora ordered his cannons to open fire on Hawaiian canoes and Olowalu Village, apparently in retaliation for the theft of a small boat. More than 100 people were senselessly killed and over 200 more were wounded near Olowalu landing, site of an ancient canoe landing. Metcalf later lost his life in a dispute with Native Americans in the Pacific Northwest. However, Metcalf's actions at Olowalu led Big Island Chief Kame'eiamoku to attack and kill the crew of the next Western ship to be seen in the islands. Ironically, that ship happened to be the Fair American, captained by Metcalf's son.

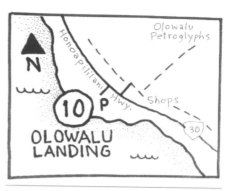

LOCATION: **Across Honoapi'ilani Highway, route 30, from the General Store. Make an immediate left after crossing the intersection and follow sign toward Camp Olowalu but then take a right where the concrete road narrows after the first split into two lines. An unmarked access road (at time of writing) leads to a small dirt parking area, the sugar mill ruins, and the canoe landing.**

The ship was attacked off Hawai'i Island and only one life was spared, that of Isaac Davis, because he faught so bravely. Davis, along with John Young (abandoned earlier by the elder Metcalf), became a trusted advisor to Kamehameha the Great. So the elder Metcalf was responsible for his son's death and played a fateful role in Hawaiian history.

The ancient canoe landing was later reinforced with a rock and concrete pier in order to serve the budding areas sugar cane industry. The first sugar crop at Olowalu was recorded in 1864 as a joint venture of King Kamehameha V, F. W. Hutchinson, and James Magee. The mill was built sometime in the 1870s and dismantled in 1933, shortly after the Olowalu Sugar Company was sold to Pioneer Mill Company. Mules and later 24 gage trains brought cane to the mill and the processed sugar was loaded on longboats at the landing to be taken to awaiting ships anchored off shore. Today, the mill site lies in ruin but the renovated canoe landing can still be appreciated. (4/55; 37; 40)

> *Ka makani ha'iha'i lau hau o Olowalu.*
> The hau-leaf tearing wind of Olowalu.
> [A gusty wind.] (28/157)
>
> —Hawaiian saying

II. **Central Maui: Wailuku**

Wailuku means "water of destruction," and may be so named because of the eighteenth century battle that took place here between the armies of Kahekili and Kalaniʻōpuʻu and/or the battle between Kamehameha I and Kalanikūpule. The slaughter was so great in the former case that Wailuku (ʻĪao) Stream was choked with the bodies of the dead and the battle was known as Kepaniwai ("the water dam"). Wailuku was also the name of an ancient chiefess, wife of Mauinui, and a sister of the Oʻahu chief Kākuhihewa.

The present-day land division of Wailuku includes all of the Central Valley between east and west Maui, as well as ʻĪao Valley and the northern portion of south Maui, Kīhei. It is the most distinctive land area in the Hawaiian Islands bordered by mountains on two opposite sides and the sea on the other two sides. Today, most of this land division is given over to agriculture, most recently the cultivation of sugar cane, as it is a fertile plain with rich volcanic soil. However, the northwestern region is home to the residential and commercial districts of Wailuku and Kahului, where Maui International Airport, the port, and the local government seat is located.

In ancient times this area around Kahului Bay was a favorite gathering place and residential site for Maui chiefs and aliʻi of high rank. From the seventeenth century it was densely populated, by Hawaiian standards, with the Pihanakalani Heiau complex serving as a spiritual

Kukuipuka Heiau in Wailuku District is one of the inaccessible heiau on private land that is cared for by a local Hawaiian group.

center. The beaches were lined with coconut groves, and along the shores were the thatched hale of fishermen and those concerned with the high chief's war canoes. Wailuku, Paukūkalo, and Waiehu were popular surfing spots for the chiefs of Maui, and from Waiheʻe to Wailuku lay the largest continuous area of wetland taro cultivation in the Islands.

The most accessible heiau in Wailuku are Halekiʻi and Pihanakalani Heiau, a double heiau complex. Human sacrifices were offered here, but only high-ranking aliʻi were the chosen victims. A Lono and a Kū Heiau can be found with a bit of a walk into the Waiheʻe Coastal Dunes and Wetlands Refuge further up the coast. Numerous other temple sites were scattered throughout this area, most of which are now destroyed. Some that survive on private property are inaccessible. Heiau names that are remembered in this area are Malaihakoa, Papanene, Poaiwa, Kealakaihonua, Kamahoe, Ka Mahoe, Ulukua, Koihale, Kapono, Kakolike, Puʻukuma, Paulani, Halelau, Malumaluakua, Puʻukoa, Kukuikomo, and Kaluli Heiau.

Kahana and Keālia Ponds are both ancient fishponds serving today as wildlife sanctuaries. Another pond, Kōʻieʻie Fishpond is a kuapā (walled) pond, which can be easily viewed from Kaʻonoʻulu Beach Park.

One of the most spectacular natural sites in the Wailuku district is ʻIao Valley State Park. It was sacred to ancient Hawaiians as a burial place for the highest-ranking aliʻi. (11; 15; 21; 22; 32; 35; 37; 39ʻ 40; 42)

> *Wailuku i ka malu he kuawa.*
> Wailuku in the shelter of valleys.
> —Hawaiian saying

ʻIao is the name of the valley within the Mauna Kahalawai Range, or West Maui Mountains. Interpretations of the name ʻIao have included "of the dawn" or "dawning inspiration," "cloud supreme," and even "mighty point (reaching to the) sky," referring to the "needle," Kūkaemoku.

Central Maui: Wailuku District Map

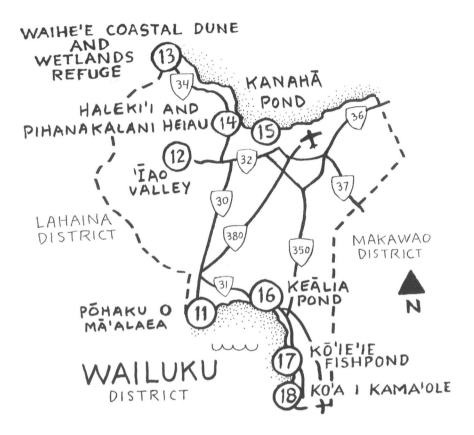

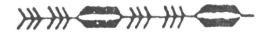

II.11 **Pōhaku o Māʻalaea**

Two boulders

Māʻalaea (possibly a contraction of Makaʻalaea, meaning "ocherous earth beginning") is the name of a village and boat harbor, a land section and bay of the same name. Adjacent to the harbor, which includes a wharf, ramp, and an adjacent ancient canoe landing, are two stones on the front lawn of the former Buzz's Wharf Restaurant. (At the time of writing the abandoned building didn't look like it would be standing much longer).

One of the stones was apparently used as a working surface for food preparation or adze grinding, and the other was apparently used in the ritual placing of piko, the umbilical cord stump of a newborn child. Pōhaku piko are common throughout Hawaiʻi, but the best-known sites lie among the large petroglyph fields on the Hawaiʻi

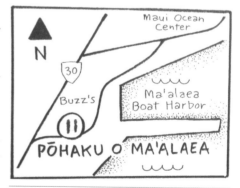

LOCATION: **Seven miles from Kahului, 15 miles from Lahaina, just off Honoapiʻilani Highway, at Māʻalaea Boat Harbor, beside the parking lot, in front of Buzz's Wharf Restaurant.**

Numerous human and dog petroglyph figures were rendered in both the linear and full-engraved-surface styles on boulders at the ancient village of Mā'alaea (after W. Walker).

Island. Leaving piko to be imbued with mana for the sake of the child was regarded as an essential practice for the health of newborns in ancient Hawai'i.

The stones were brought to Mā'alaea in 1952 from an old village site above Manu'ōhule ("bird [of the] meeting point of receding and incoming waves"), not far from McGregor Point. A number of boulders near the village heiau have petroglyphs carved on them. Numerous human and dog figures are fashioned in both the linear and full-engraved-surface styles. Boulders from this village were used in the construction of the breakwater at Mā'alaea Boat Harbor, but, when it was discovered that the ancient village was being destroyed to provide building materials, these two pōhaku were saved from the fate of hundreds of others. They stand at their present location as a reminder of all the ancient sites that have disappeared in order that new sites might be established.

Also in the Mā'alaea vicinity was a heiau and an ancient spring called Kapoli, which means "the bosom." However, the spring has since dried up. (4/51; 32/89,137, 146; 37/21-23; 40)

II.12 'Īao Valley

Natural features

'Īao is the name of a small fish, a bird, and the planet Jupiter when it appears as a morning star. However, 'Īao is most known as the name of the valley and peak ("needle rock"), in the Mauna Kahalawai range, or West Maui Mountains. Interpretations of the name 'Īao have been "of the dawn" or "dawning inspiration," in reference to the morning's life-giving sunshine that was kapu at this place to all but Maui ali'i. Or it may mean "cloud supreme," as indicative of the regular presence of protective cloud covering in this valley. "Mighty point (reaching to the)

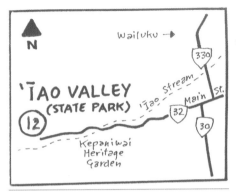

LOCATION: **At the west, mauka end of Main Street (Hwy. 32), 5 miles from the center of Wailuku.**

sky" is another likely meaning and may specifically refer to the "needle," Kūkaemoku.

Ancient prophecy warned that the Maui kingdom and way of life would end forever if an enemy succeeded in entering ʻĪao Valley. The valley had been designated as kapu and a sacred burial ground by paramount chief Kākaʻe in the 1400s and all worthy Maui aliʻi were buried in the valley up until the time of Kahekili. Kākaʻe lived in seclusion in the valley because even a glance at him by a commoner would break a powerful kapu punishable by death, and the chief wished not to condemn his people to such a fate. His cave is said to be adjacent to the present public parking area in ʻĪao Valley State Park. A large boulder called Ka Pili o Kākaʻe, and referred to as "the champion of Kākaʻe," stood in front of the cave entrance and supposedly made the chief invisible to others. The boulder was shown great respect by Hawaiians until it was pushed into the stream, where a flash flood later moved it downstream. Only a few local residents know the present location of Ka Pili o Kākaʻe.

Common people were allowed to enter the otherwise kapu valley only during the four-month winter season of Makahiki that began with the rising of Makaliʻi (the Pleiades) in the evening skies. Honoring the god Lono, the people could partake of shrimp, fish, taro, and other specialties of the valley once they traveled up Kinihāpai ("uplifting of the multitude") Stream, which flows by Kūkaemoku ("broken excrement"). The aliʻi would travel a different route into the valley, up Wailuku Stream, formerly known as Kepela Stream, past Ka Pili o Kākaʻe.

In the summer of 1790, Kamehameha the Great attacked central Maui. One tradition indicates that Kamehameha's war canoes landed at Kalepolepo near Keālia Pond from where he proceeded inland toward Wailuku. The four streams of this region tell the story of the unfolding battle. Kamehameha placed a kapu on the first stream he came to reserving it for aliʻi. Waikapū ("water of the conch") was where the sacred conch shell was blown sounding the call to war. At Wailuku ("water of destruction") Stream, the battle became fierce and many warriors were killed. The Maui armies were routed and took flight by way of the third stream, Waiehu ("water spray"), kicking up the water in a frenzied dash to get away. By Waiheʻe ("squid liquid") Stream the Maui army was utterly defeated and simply melted away like the ink of a fleeing octopus.

However, another description of this decisive battle speaks of a land-

Near the entrance of ʻĪao Valley is the Kepaniwai Heritage Gardens in which Ahu Kinihapai ("Uplifting of the Multitude") may be seen. This ahu (altar) was dedicated on January 20, 2013 to honor those who stood against the illegal overthrow of the Hawaiian Kingdom on January 16, 1893 and the annexation of Hawaiʻi by the United States in 1897.

ing at the Kawela area of Kahului Bay, perhaps a second wave, where two days of fighting into ʻĪao Valley took place. Here, with the help of a cannon, a terrible slaughter of commoners took place and in such great numbers that the dead bodies dammed up the water of Wailuku Stream. It has been referred to as Kepaniwai, or "the water dam." From here people fled to Kauwaʻupali ("precipice climbers" or "clawed of the cliff"), past ʻĪao Needle, scrambling up the steep cliffs at the back of the valley to escape. Women, children, and the elderly fled up the gulch called Aʻi, now known as Black Gorge. Chief Kalanikūpule and other Maui aliʻi are said to have escaped over the pali (cliff) to Lahaina, where they secured canoes and fled to Oʻahu.

Facing the valley entrance, Mauna Kāne is the peak on the right, named after one of the major Hawaiian gods. On the left is Mauna Leo, meaning "voice mountain," which, according to one source was changed to Līʻō ("terror") after the invasion by Kamehameha. This fight between the armies of Hawaiʻi and those of Maui is now known as the Battle of ʻĪao.

The summit of the needle, Kūkaemoku, reaches 2,250 feet above sea level and is said to be the body of the legendary handsome youth who seduced ʻĪao, the beautiful daughter of Hina. Another tale tells of a beautiful maiden called, ironically, Luahinepiʻi ("climbing old woman"), who lived in ʻĪao canyon and was teased by other maidens who were jealous of her good looks. As Luahinepiʻi had an unpleasant sounding voice, the other maidens started a false rumor that her lover disapproved of her voice. Humiliated, she climbed the phallic rock Kūkaemoku, also called Nānāhoa, and cast herself headfirst to the valley below, her voice never to be heard again. The needle is also associated with Kanaloa, Hawaiian god of the ocean.

The West Maui Mountains, Mauna Kahalawai, which form the crescent-shaped valley of ʻĪao, are also known as Halemahina, ("the house of the moon"). They stand in contrast to Haleakalā, ("the house of the sun"). Two miles into the valley is the Maui County Park, Kepaniwai Heritage Gardens, and a little further on is ʻĪao Valley State Park. (32, 37/79-85; 40)

> *Ka pali kāohi kumu aliʻi o ʻĪao.*
> The cliff of ʻĪao that embraces the chiefly sources.
> [ʻĪao, Maui, was the burial place of many chiefs of high
> rank who are the ancestors of living chiefs.] (28/165)
> —Hawaiian saying

II.13 **Waiheʻe**

(Coastal Dunes and Wetlands Refuge)
Coastal wetland area with archaeological features

The Waiheʻe Coastal Dunes and Wetlands Refuge is an important natural preserve and a significant cultural site in central Maui. Now a 277-acre habitat for wildlife and native vegetation, the preserve was once the site of two thriving ancient Maui fishing villages, an extensive inland fishpond, and 93 other archaeological features including heiau. The villages are now gone but house site foundations are still visible. The fishpond is mostly dried up and unproductive but still spring-fed and wet in the rainy season. A coastal heiau, referred to by locals as a Lono temple, is still remembered and viewable. This structure of water-worn stones is Kealakaʻihonua Heiau. Attributed to Koi, a priest of the Kaleopuʻupuʻu order, a high-ranking group of chiefs of Kahekili. Koi is believed to have been involved in the deaths of

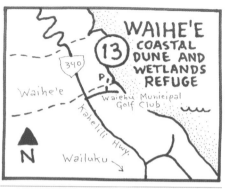

LOCATION: **Eight miles from Kahului, take Kahului Beach Road to Waiehu Beach Road (Route 340) and turn right on Halewaiu Road after the Waiehu Golf Course and before Waiheʻe Elementary School. Drive down to where the road forks to the right for the golf course parking but turn left on the less obvious dirt road, cross the shallow stream (only if its low) and park under the trees and walk into the gated area to the left. Follow the unpaved road on foot, past the abandoned house on the right and the houses on the left to the start of the footpath into the open area of the preserve.**

two British officers and a seaman from Captain Vancouver's Daedalus landing at Waimea on Oʻahu in 1795. Kealakaʻihonua Heiau was rededicated by Kamehameha the Great in 1802, in preparation for his invasion of Kauaʻi. Archaeologist Winslow Walker described the heiau in the early 1930s as consisting of a "series of platforms and terraces extending back some 150 feet from the waters edge." Terraced features are no longer distinguishable.

The fishpond, which occupied the center of the refuge, was of the loko iʻa kalo type and was about 6-acres in size. Ancient Hawaiians combined loko (pond) and kalo (taro) in a perfect integration of fishing and farming. Wetland kalo was grown in loʻi (paddies), shallow ponds that were also used to raise fish. Abundant rainfall in the Mauna Kahalawai, West Maui Mountains, provided fresh water irrigation to the loʻi. In ancient times Waiheʻe was a very productive agricultural area growing mostly wetland kalo (taro). Nine kalo patches are under restoration within the refuge in an effort to promote Community Supported Agriculture in the area. Having been cleared and resorted for habitat-appropriate plants the wetlands are now home to aeʻo (stilts), alae keʻokeʻo (coot), koloa (duck), and nene (goose).

Kapoho village was between the fishpond and the ocean, and would

Kealakaihonua Heiau, attributed to Koi, a priest of the Kaleopuʻupuʻu order in the ranks of Kahekili, is constructed of water-worn stones and originally had terraced platforms.

have been constructed with rock foundations, wood frames, and pili grass thatch. Stone foundations can still be seen in places. Kapoho was at one time the temporary home of Piʻilani, the first mōʻī or paramount chief to unite all of Maui Island. This spot was also the scene of the battle of Kalaeʻiliʻili between Kahahana and Keʻeaumoku. Both aliʻi lived in Waiheʻe and Kahahana led a rebellion against Keʻeaumoku for the latter not fairly distributing fish to the people. Lasting several days in 1765 the battle ended with Keʻeaumoku and his wife Namahana fleeing to Hawaiʻi Island where he later joined forces with Kamehameha the Great.

This part of Waiheʻe is an example of one of the last undeveloped sand dune systems in the area. On all of the islands Hawaiians used such dunes as burial grounds. Originally slated for golf course development, the area became the Waiheʻe Coastal Dunes and Wetlands Refuge with the help of funding by Maui County ($2M), the United States Fish and Wildlife Service ($2M), and the National Oceanic and Atmospheric Administration ($800k), and with oversight and ownership by the Hawaiian Islands Land Trust. (37; 40)

Pictured is a possible kuʻula or fishing shrine with Haleakalā shrouded in cloud in the background.

II.14 **Haleki'i-Pihanakalani Heiau**

Two rock temple foundations

Haleki'i ("house of images") and Pihanakalani ("fullness [of] the heavens") Heiau are credited to the building skills of menehune (legendary race of small people), who, according to legend, could construct ancient stone structures in one night by passing rocks hand-to-hand over great distances. It seems that these stones were carried up from Paukūkalo ("taro piece") Beach, not far away. Another tradition associates the heiau with the West Maui high chief Ki'ikewa, who lived at "the time of Kāka'e." The temples were dedicated as heiau luakini for the sacrifice of only high chiefs and ali'i of the purest lineage.

Maui's paramount chief, Kahekili, set up court here after his father came to the heiau to die in

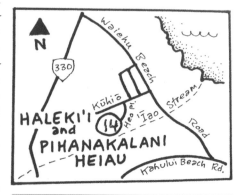

LOCATION: Take Kahului Beach Road to Waiehu Beach Road (Route 340), just beyond the 'Īao Stream bridge, turn left onto Kūhiō Place. Turn left again on Heo Place, marked by a Hawai'i Visitors Bureau sign, and drive uphill to parking lot.

1736. Just outside the temple precinct, the warriors of Kahekili practiced boxing, as well as other war games. Keōpūolani, a high-ranking chiefess of both Maui and Hawai'i Island lineage, was born here at Pihanakalani. She became the wife of Kamehameha I and the mother of Liholiho (Kamehameha II) and Kauikeaouli (Kamehameha III). In 1790, as he strove to unite the Hawaiian Islands, Kamehameha I defeated the Maui warriors of Kalanikūpule at the nearby battle of 'Īao Valley. Following this decisive battle, Kamehameha, honoring his war god, offered the last human sacrifice at Haleki'i. Kalani-Kauko'olua'ole, a Maui chiefess who Kamehameha felt had offended him at Kaupō, was sent for, but her foster-sister Poloahilani stepped forward as a substitute and was sacrificed instead.

In 1819, following the death of Kamehameha I, Pihanakalani was demolished by Kalanimakauali'i and Kauanaulu according to the proclamation of Ka'ahumanu, widow of Kamehameha. All of the sacred images at Haleki'i were destroyed. Since then, erosion has further contributed to the ruin of the site. During World War II a road and waterline were constructed across the heiau, with a water tank placed on Haleki'i and a bunker built into Pihanakalani. Restoration of the heiau was carried out by the Maui Historical Society in 1958, and the area was acquired by the State of Hawai'i in 1959. The water tank has since been removed, the bunker has been covered, and further improvements have been made to bring the area back to its near-original condition. Haleki'i and Pihanakalani Heiau together are now designated as an official state monument called Haleki'i-Pihana Heiau State Historic Site.

The monument lies along the 'Īao Stream, between 'Īao Valley and Kahului Harbor. The two heiau stand on a sand dune, from which one has panoramic views in all directions. Haleki'i Heiau was "reserved for the females of high rank," and was probably surrounded by wooden ki'i, as its name, "house of images" suggests. The Bishop Museum has a wooden image found in a taro patch below Haleki'i, probably from the

Haleki'i Heiau was probably surrounded by wooden ki'i, as its name, "house of images" suggests. One hundred yards mauka of Haleki'i is Pihanakalani Heiau. Pihanakalani often refers to the entire double-temple complex, which was used as a heiau luakini or human sacrifice temple at least from the time of Kahekili.

Haleki'i-Pihana Heiau State Historic Site consists of two heiau standing on a sand dune ridge above 'Īao Stream, from which one has panoramic views in all directions. Mauna Kahalawai and 'Īao Valley stand behind the monument and the stream and ocean lie below and in front of it.

heiau. The heiau lu-apua'u (refuse pit) was called Liliha, and was said to lead to a cave below the heiau. Hale-ki'i, the more north-erly of the two tem-ples, is three hundred feet long from north to south and 150 feet wide from east to west. On the prominent east-ern side one can see the impressive stone-work of stacked, water-worn boulders, forming small enclosures and depressions. The level top of Haleki'i is now covered with grass, but excavations have shown that just below the sur-face a fine 'ili'ili stone paving is hidden. This heiau was apparently once called Kalola.

One hundred yards mauka of Haleki'i, along a trail, is Pihanakalani Heiau. This temple is about 300 feet in length from north to south, with a sharp bow-like corner pointing toward its sister heiau. Pihanakalani, also built of large beach stones, has a 166-foot by 90-foot court lying perpendicular to the central structure. Pihanakalani often refers to the entire double-temple complex, which was used as a heiau luakini at least from the time of Kahekili, but perhaps even earlier. It was an im-portant focal point for both religious and political power in the Wailuku area and for all of West Maui.

Excavations carried out in 1989–90 found that Pihanakalani was originally a small temple built between 1260 and 1400. By 1640 it had been expanded and used as an ali'i residence. It was during this second building phase that Haleki'i was constructed. Both temples underwent renovations in the late 1600s. Between 1684 and 1778, Pihanakalani Hei-au was expanded and reoriented to face the island of Hawai'i, probably in response to the wars being fought with that neighbor island at the time. Human bones, as well as pig and fish bones, have been found at the heiau. Five major building episodes and ten minor phases took place here.

During the 1990s the double heiau site suffered damage caused by a local company quarrying sand along its ancient hillside foundations. The park had at one time several informational signs for visitors and plans to upgrade the quality of the state monument but at the time of writing this revised edition Haleki'i-Pihanakalani Heiau State Historic Site was looking very neglected. (11; 20; 21/66-67; 32; 35; 37/75-78; 40; 42)

II.15 **Kanahā Pond**

(State Wildlife Sanctuary)
Wetland area

Kanahā ("the shattered [thing]") Pond was formerly a royal fish-pond believed to have been built by chief Kihaapiʻilani, who lived about 1500 and was the son of Piʻilani. Another tradition attributes the building of the pond to Kapiʻiohoʻokalani, a high chief of Oʻahu and Molokaʻi. He is said to have brought many men to build the double ponds of Kanahā and Mauʻoni. It was constructed by passing stones hand-to-hand from Makawela. However, the great chief did not live to dedi-

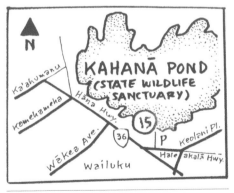

LOCATION: **Off Haleakalā Hwy. (Route 396) near the junction of Hāna Hwy. (Route 36).**

cate the ponds. This was done by his daughter, Kahamaluihiikeaoihilani, who named one of them for her brother Kanahāokalani. Wetland taro was cultivated in this area of Wailuku, and fish were often raised within the taro ponds themselves. By the seventeenth century Wailuku was well populated, and a favorite gathering place of chiefs. Pond fish were generally reserved for ali'i, and the kuapā (dividing wall) that separated these two ponds was kapu to commoners.

No longer a maintained fishpond, Kanahā is a State Wildlife Sanctuary. Declared a wildlife refuge in 1952 and a Registered National History Landmark in 1971, the pond is home to some fifty species of birds, including coots, doves, ducks, gallinules, geese, herons, owls, pheasants, plovers, sandpipers, and tattlers. However, the sanctuary is best known as the part-time residence of the migratory āe'o, or Hawaiian stilt. Nearly 500 of

Kanahā Pond Wildlife Sanctuary, between the Kahului airport and the harbor, was at one time a productive royal fishpond whose fish were reserved for ali'i.

the endangered āe'o have been counted here at one time, an estimated one-third of the known population.

Kanahā Pond and its wildlife are best viewed from a paved walkway and observation shelter at the south end of the refuge. A few Hawaiian plants have been reintroduced along the walkway and beside the parking lot. Remember to keep the gate closed. (4/9; 32/83; 37/87)

> *Pākāhi ka nehu a Kapi'ioho.*
> The nehu of Kapi'ioho are divided, one to a person.
> [Kapi'ioho, ruler of Moloka'i, had two ponds, Mau'oni and Kanahā, built on his land at Kahului, Maui. The men who were brought from Moloka'i and O'ahu to build the ponds were fed on food brought over from Moloka'i. The drain on that island was often so great that the men were reduced to eating nehu fish, freshwater 'ōpae and poi. The saying is used when poi is plentiful but fish is scarce and has to be carefully rationed.] (28/284)
> —Hawaiian saying

11.16 **Keālia Pond**

(National Wildlife Refuge)
Coastal wetland area

Keālia means "the salt encrustation," and was known for its "most excellent salt," made from the saltpans in the immediate vicinity. It is also the name and site of a former fishpond. Little is known about the ancient history of Keālia fishpond, but, judging from its size, it must have been an important producer of fish stock, particularly awa (milkfish) and ʻamaʻama (mullet). Ditches and sluice gates were built at least 400 years ago to let these and other nearshore fish into the

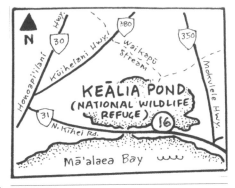

LOCATION: **Between Kīhei and Māʻalaea, on both sides of North Kīhei Road, Route 31.**

pond. A koʻa (fishing shrine) or possible heiau platform stands near the site. Separated from the ocean by Māʻalaea Beach, the pond is fed by streams from both sides of the island and its water level continually fluctuates throughout the year. The size of Keālia Pond is noticeably in-

Separated from the ocean by Māʻalaea Beach, the pond is fed by streams from both sides of the island and its water level continually fluctuates throughout the year.

creased by the flow from Waikapū ("water [of] the conch") Stream, originating in the West Maui Mountains, and from Kolaloa ("much sexual excitement") Gulch, coming from the slopes of Haleakalā.

The area was used by the 2nd and 4th Marine Divisions as a training site during World War II. Since 1992, Keālia Pond has been a part of the Wildlife Refuge System, overseen by the U.S. Fish and Wildlife Service. The 691-acre bird sanctuary attracts 30 species of birds, including waterfowl, shorebirds and migratory ducks, particularly in the winter when the pond becomes a wetland paradise. The endangered aeʻo and ʻalae keʻokeʻo can be seen here at certain times of year. The refuge has added some publicly accessible ponds called Kanuimanu Ponds. Also, a 4,400-foot boardwalk along part of the southern part of the refuge, a bridge over the pond outlet, a kiosk, outdoor classrooms, and a parking lot have been constructed. The best time to visit is between August and April, when the birds are not nesting.

For more information, visit the refuge headquarters off Mokulele Highway (Hwy. 31) outside of Kīhei near milepost 6, (808) 875-1582, www.fws.gov/kealiapond, or write to: Keālia Pond N.W.R., P.O. Box 1042, Kīhei, HI 96753. Open weekdays 7:30 AM to 4 PM but call ahead as the Visitors Center is often closed. (18/17, 37/95; 41)

II.17 **Kōʻieʻie Fishpond**

Coastal fishpond ruins

In ancient times at least three or four kuapā (walled) fishponds were built along the Kīhei ("cloak") coastline. With the exception of Kōʻieʻie pond, the names of the other ponds have been lost, and little is known about any of their histories. In such cases it was said the menehune were their builders.

Kōʻieʻie Fishpond, in Kaʻonoʻulu ("the desire for breadfruit") Park, is located along Kalepolepo ("the dirt") Beach and is on both the National and State Registries of Historical Sites. Kalepolepo probably got its name from the dirt and dust clouds that are kicked up in this area due to the strong winds funneled through the Central Valley. One can still experience this wind and its dirt clouds during the winter months. The coastal

LOCATION: At Kaʻonoʻulu Beach County Park, along South Kīhei Road, between the office of the Hawaiian Island Humpback Whale National Marine Sanctuary and the Menehune Shores apartment building.

The Captain Vancouver Monument is a quarter mile up the beach from Kōʻieʻie Fishpond. Vancouver, who sailed with the British naval Captain James Cook on the first recorded European voyage to the Hawaiian Islands, stopped at Kīhei on his own later voyage.

area here is also known as Ka Ipu Kai a Hina, ("the meat dish of Hina,") and may point to the abundance of fresh fish that fishponds provided in this region. At Kōʻieʻie Fishpond one can still see the occasional fisherman trying to catch pāpio (young jackfish) by pole or by net.

It is here at Kalepolepo that Kamehameha I is said to have beached his canoes for battle against Central Maui. The beaches were black with his fleet, and the Waikapū Stream that empties into nearby Keālia Pond was declared kapu. Later, Kamehameha, who noticed Kōʻieʻie to be in disrepair, had the fishpond rebuilt. It is recorded that chief ʻUmilīloa, in the mid-1500s, also had the pond walls rebuilt. For this reason and that of its size this fishpond is believed to have been a royal pond always stocked with the best fish.

In 1815, one of King Kamehameha's sons died at Kalepolepo. Kihawahine, the family ʻaumakua, who had her residence at Loko Mokuhinia in Lahaina, is said to have appeared at Kōʻieʻie Fishpond dressed in yellow and saffron colored kapa (paper cloth). Kōʻieʻie is a loko kuapā ("walled pond") that had one mākāhā (sluice gate). It is a small pond of three acres. At low tide, another fishpond ruin can be seen just south of Kōʻieʻie Fishpond, and still further south along the coast is yet another nameless ancient pond wall. A plaque at the entrance to the park commemorates this ancient site and its legendary neighborhood.

Historic sites such as the Captain Vancouver Monument and David Malo's Kilolani Church are a quarter mile and a half mile away, respectively. Vancouver was one of the early European explorers who, after sailing to the Islands with the British naval Captain James Cook, later made his own voyages, which included a stop at Kīhei. He was the first European to land at Maui. David Malo, a respected authority on island cultural history, was a Native Hawaiian Christian minister who in traditional Hawaiian fashion called his congregation to services by blowing a conch shell. His unique outdoor church, built in 1853, is covered only by overhanging kiawe branches.

There are plans to restore Kōʻieʻie Fishpond for use as an educational and recreational site. For further information contact: ʻAoʻao o Nā Loko Iʻa o Maui (Association for the Fishponds of Maui), 726 South Kīhei Road, Kīhei, Maui, HI 96753. (4/47; 32/77, 86; 37/250)

Kōʻieʻie is a 3-acre loko kuapā ("walled pond") that had only one mākāhā (sluice gate). At low tide, another fishpond ruin can be seen just south of Kōʻieʻie Fishpond.

11.18 **Koʻa i Kamaʻole**

Fishing shrine

Koʻa i Kamaʻole ("childless fish shrine") is a site that was discovered during the construction of the Kīhei Public Library. This low stone platform between the sidewalk and the parking lot is filled with white coral fragments, which alerted archaeologists to the type of site known as a koʻa or fishing shrine.

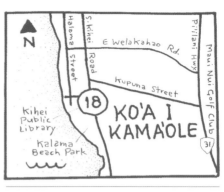

LOCATION: **35 Waimahaihai Street, in Kīhei, 96753, off South Kīhei Road.**

Such stone structures, which could even be a small heiau (place of ritual practice), an ahu (altar), or upright pōhaku (sacred stone), are normally found near favorite fishing grounds, streams, or ponds. The first catch of the day was left at a koʻa as an offering of thanks to the god or goddess, and trust that the offering would help to continue a plentiful supply. Koʻa were a residence for a spirit helpful to fishermen. Kūʻula was the most prominent Hawaiian fish god and he was said to speak to fishermen through dreams, directing them to good fishing grounds and a healthy life.

Koʻa i Kamaʻole means the "childless fish shrine" in Hawaiian and is a site that was discovered during the construction of the Kīhei Public Library. It is a low stone platform filled with white coral fragments, typical of fishing shrines.

III. **South Maui & Upcountry: Makawao**

Makawao ("forest beginning") is the large land section that includes the former Haʻikū districts of Hāmākuapoko and Hāmākualoa, the district of Kula, and the land division of Honuaʻula ("red land"). It encompasses most of the western slope of Haleakalā from the summit and western interior of the crater, to the eastern edge of the central plain, from the northern Haʻikū shores to the South Maui coastline of Kīhei and Kamaʻole. Most of the temperate region of upcountry pastures and homesteads is referred to today as Kula ("open country"). There are a number of petroglyph and pictograph sites here in the rocky gulches, but these are on private land and not accessible.

Down on the dry leeward coast, from Wailea to Keoneʻōʻio, ancient fishing and farming settlements once dotted the region. Although resort development has taken over Wailea, its ancient sites can be better understood if one hikes through the La Perouse Historic District. Here, unrestored archaeological features are seen in more or less their original settings.

The green, forested paniolo (cowboy) country of Makawao eventually gives way to the rocky and barren higher elevations of Haleakalā. Inside the crater there is no sign of permanent habitation by ancient Hawaiians, but regular visits for religious and ceremonial reasons did take place over the course of many centuries and some remnants of these visits are still visible. (1; 4; 8; 15; 20; 37; 40)

In the upcountry region known as Kula ("open country") are a number of petroglyph and pictograph sites. In the rocky gulches, usually on inaccessible private property, these kiʻi pōhaku usually depict human and animal figures. This pictograph is painted rather than etched into the rock outcrop.

Resort development has taken over much of South Maui but the La Perouse Historic District offers the opportunity to see unrestored archaeological sites in more or less their original settings.

Keiki holoholo kuāua o Makawao.
The lad of Makawao who goes about in the rain.
[Said of a native of that place who is not afraid of being wet.] (31/ 184)
—Hawaiian saying

South Maui and Upcountry: Makawao District Map

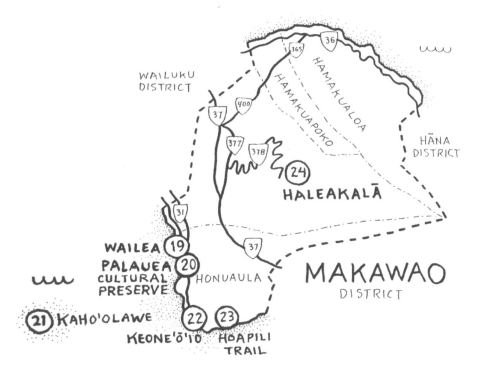

III.19 **Wailea**

Rock wall enclosures

Wailea means "water belonging to Lea," and Lea was known both as a fish deity and as a goddess of canoe makers. This area was certainly suited to both activities of fishing and canoe building, for the sea is an important resource at Wailea. Offshore fishing was a major occupation in ancient Wailea, where even today there is an abundant supply of iʻa (fish and seafood of all kinds), including limu (seaweed), wana (sea urchins), pāpaʻi (crabs), ula (lobster), pūpū (shellfish), and honu (turtle). Whales are often spotted just off-shore here during their season (January to March). In addition to harvesting the fruits of the sea, early Hawaiians cultivated taro, sweet potato, coconut, kukui trees and many other useful crops just upland from the coast.

Because of its plentiful natural resources, Wailea was home to a stable farming and fishing community. The coastline from Wailea, through Kahikinui to Hāna, was apparently one of the most populated regions of Maui for at least five centuries, beginning from about 1350. The region of Wailea was not a seat of royalty and, therefore, its people lived

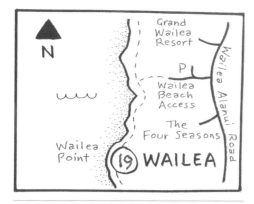

LOCATION: **From Wailea Shopping Center, go .4 miles south on Wailea Alanui to Wailea Beach access between the Grand Wailea Resort and The Four Seasons. Continue south on foot, along a paved coastal path about one-half mile to the ancient site at Wailea Point, from which Molokini may also be viewed.**

simply and peacefully avoided the power struggles and bloody battles that plagued Lahaina, Wailuku, and Hāna.

Today this entire coastal area is given over in large part to resort development. Although few ancient Hawaiian ruins remain in Wailea, some hotels have small displays of artifacts collected from their construction sites. At Wailea Point two partially restored residential hale and a large ʻiliʻili stone-paved "working area" can be seen. The two restored rock-wall enclosures were used by Hawaiian villagers for sleeping and storage, and perhaps as a "boarding house" for fishermen and travelers. Over 600 artifacts were recovered from this site, half of which were pre-contact items such as stone adze heads, poi pounders, coral abraders, fishhooks, sinkers, and fish bones. Some early contact artifacts found within the enclosures were American silver coins, a Chinese ceramic whiskey bottle, German wine bottles, English ceramic and clay pipes, and a French cologne bottle. A little more than a century after the arrival of westerners in Hawaiʻi, disease, change in lifestyle, and redirection of spiritual orientation forced the Hawaiians to abandon Wailea, and many other villages like it. Near the restored stone enclosures was an ancient spring, which dried up only recently.

From Wailea one has

At Wailea Point two partially restored residential hale and a large ʻiliʻili stone-paved "working area" can be found. There is a good view from here of the cinder cone of Puʻu ʻŌlaʻl (left), the crescent-shaped offshore island Molokini, and the uninhabited island of Kahoʻolawe.

a good view of Molokini, a crescent-shaped offshore island. Born the daughter of Pu'uhele and Pu'uokali, Molokini's given name was Pu'uoin-aina and she was a mo'o (lizard) as her parents were. She married Lo-hi'au, Pele's dream-lover, who stayed at Mā'alaea. When the volcano goddess heard of this, she cursed Pu'uoinaina, who in fear and shame cast herself into the ocean. Pele, coming from Kahikinui, happened upon Pu'uoinaina in the water and cut off her head, which became Pu'uolai ("earthquake hill") at Mākena, and severed her tail, which be-came the islet of Molokini. When Lohi'au saw part of his beloved floating in the sea, he called it Molokini, meaning "many ties." Another tradition speaks of the island of Maui as the figure of a woman with Molokini as her piko (belly button). During World War II the U.S. Navy used Moloki-ni for live ammunition exercises. Bomb craters and ordnance fragments are still found on the island, which is now a bird sanctuary and marine preserve. (18/ 54-58; 37/233; 40)

III.20 **Palauea Cultural Preserve**
Village and heiau ruins

Palauea is an ahupuaʻa (land area) in the traditional moku (large land division) of Honuaʻula, and the Makawao District (also called Kula), between Kīhei and Mākena.

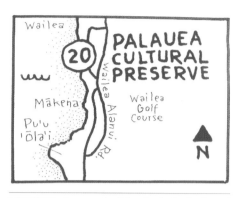

The first archaeological survey of Palauea was done in 1969 and it recognized the cultural significance of the area, especially the Palauea Heiau Complex. Radiocarbon testing indicated charcoal dates as early as 370 CE and permanent settlement between AD 1480 and 1890. The region was amply populated and farmed while the coastal areas were utilized by fishing communities.

LOCATION: **Access to this site is limited and by arrangement only. Contact the Office of Hawaiian Affairs (873-3364).**

The present-day site includes heiau (places of ritual practice), hale (house site foundations, ahu (cairns), agricultural terraces, and foot trails. Evidence of fishing activities can be found along the coast. Remnants of historic-era ranching are also visible. Some 16 site complexes with 255 features have been documented.

In the 1970s landowners and developers were interested in the area for resort and residential development. As preservation relies primarily on landowner's consent, many koʻa (fishing shrines) and ancient house sites were bulldozed as properties were subdi-

Palauea Cultural Preserve includes a heiau (places of ritual practice), hale (house site) foundations, ahu (cairns), agricultural terraces, and foot trails. Sixteen site complexes with 255 features have been documented on the 20.75 acre site.

vided and sold during this time. In 1998 the Kīhei-Mākena Community Plan formed the Palauea Cultural Preserve in order to save the heiau complex as an historic park. In 1999, in order to get approval for 18 single-family residential lots, land developer Dowling Company set aside 20.75 acres (Lot 18) for the Palauea Cultural Preserve.

Now surrounded by multimillion-dollar homes, the Preserve was stewarded by Dowling, Co. However, the Office of Hawaiian Affairs has recently taken ownership of the Preserve and put into place a unique arrangement whereby every time a lot is sold or resold .5% of the sale price goes into a fund to manage Palauea Cultural Preserve. OHA is presently putting together a management plan together with its partner the University of Hawai'i Maui College that will use the site as a "living classroom." The fund already has $230,000. UH Maui College Hawaiian Studies Department, the new steward of the property, has had access to the site for archaeological field studies, and involvement by the local community is also part of the desired management program. The site also includes a 900-square-foot building, the former Dowling sales office, which will be converted into a classroom. (32; 37; 40)

III.21 **Kahoʻolawe**

Island

(Wikimedia Commons)

From the coastal area of Kīhei in South Maui and from upcountry Kula in the Makawao District, a stunning view of low-lying Kahoʻolawe can be had. Although it is clearly a separate island, Kahoʻolawe (7 miles from Maui) was traditionally considered a part of Maui's Honuaʻula moku (larger land division) and it is therefore included here as a independent site of Maui even though access is limited.

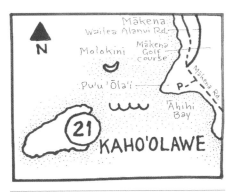

Kaho'olawe is 11 miles long and 6 miles wide, with a total land area of 45 square miles. The highest point on the island is the summit of Pu'u Moaulanui on Lua Makika crater at a height of 1,477 feet above sea level. It is now mostly a dry, barren landscape due to the Hawaiian chiefs paying off their debts to western traders in sandalwood exports. The resulting deforestation adversely affected the rainfall pattern on Maui and it's smaller neighbor island. Kaho'olawe is in the rain shadow of eastern Maui's 10,023-foot Haleakalā.

LOCATION: **Access to the island is limited and by arrangement only. Contact the Kaho'olawe Island Reserve Commission, 811 Kolu Street, Suite 201, Wailuku, HI 96793. (808) 243-5020, administrator@ kirc.hawaii.gov**

Kaho'olawe was home to an important ancient resource at Pu'u Moiwi, a remnant cinder cone, where the second largest basalt quarry in Hawai'i was located. Basalt was necessary for making ko'i, or adze hammers. Ancient house sites, heiau platforms and enclosures, ahu, and petroglyphs are reminders of the early settlements here.

Hawai'i Island High Chief Kalani'ōpu'u raided the island as part of his many attempts to conquer Maui. European sailors of the late 18th and early 19th centuries described Kaho'olawe as a desolate and uninhabited place. Kamehameha III replaced the death penalty in the 1830s with exile to Kaho'olawe, making it into a penal colony until 1853. In the late 1850s there were 50 residents subsisting on the produce from small shoreline gardens. The Hawaiian government then leased the island for ranching, which led to over-grazing and severe erosion. After Hawai'i became an American territory in 1898, a reforestation plan failed to revive the island in the early 20th century. In 1913 John Stokes of the Bishop Museum together with a team of archaeologists carried out surveys on the island and in 1931 Gilbert McAllister, also of the Bishop Museum, published *Archaeology of Kaho'olawe* after a week-long survey that detailed 50 ancient sites on the island.

When America entered WWII, martial law was declared and Kaho'olawe was taken over for military training including torpedo and bombing practice. In 1953 President Eisenhower confirmed the military's need to use the island with the proviso that when it was no longer needed, the island would be returned in a condition "suitable for human habitation." Hawai'i became a state in 1959 and bombing was temporarily halted in 1969 when a 500 lb. unexploded bomb was found

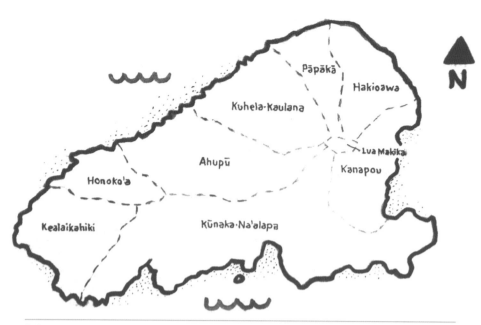

Kohemālamalama, which means "bright vagina," is the old Hawaiian name for the island of Kahoʻolawe. There are nine traditional ahupuaʻa or land divisions.

in a west Maui field. In 1976 the Protect Kahoʻolawe ʻOhana (PKO) was formed. Nine members of the ʻOhana landed on the island in protest, and a federal lawsuit was filed against the U.S. Navy for violating laws pertaining to religious freedom, historic preservation, and the environment. In 1977 PKO members Kimo Mitchell and George Helm were lost at sea off Kahoʻolawe while protesting the military's use, and the U.S. Federal Court ordered the Department of Defense to conduct an inventory of the island's ancient sites.

Some 540 archaeological sites were thus documented and Kahoʻolawe was declared a National Historical District in 1981. Over 4,500 artifacts and 2,081 historical features were mapped by 2001, and some 10,000 historical items were found by the end of the cleanup period. In 1992 the Kahoʻolawe Island Reserve Commission (KIRC) was established and in 1993 the U.S. Congress voted to end military use of the island and set aside $400 million for the removal of ordnance. Munitions clearing ceased in 2004 with only 75% of the island declared safe and accessible.

Visits to the island are restricted and limited to officially arranged travel, however volunteer opportunities are available in the form of monthly, 3-day restoration work camps (see KIRC website: www.kahoolawe.hawaii.gov). When visiting groups arrive at Kahoʻolawe they recite the following chant (There is another chant for departing the island).

Oli Kāhea

He haki nu'anu'a nei kai
'O 'awa ana I uka
Pehea e hiki aku ai
'O ka leo
Mai pa'a I ka leo.

Entry Chant

Indeed a rough and crashing sea
Echoing into the uplands
How is it that one lands?
It is the voice
Do not hold back the voice.

When the Kaho'olawe Island Reserve Commission was established it was stated that the entire island and its coastal waters would only be used for Native Hawaiian cultural, spiritual, and subsistence purposes—environmental restoration, historic preservation, and education. It would not be used for any commercial purposes. When the U.S. Navy officially returned the title of the island to the State of Hawai'i in 1994, it was also promised by all the parties involved "to be held in trust until the formation of a federally-recognized sovereign Hawaiian entity."

Kaho'olawe means "the carrying away (by currents)" and was believed to be an important long-distance navigational site for early Hawaiians. There is a navigational heiau on the island and a stretch of ocean southwest of the island is called Kealaikahiki, "the Road to Tahiti." Kohemālamalama, which means "bright vagina," was the old Hawaiian name for the island of Kaho'olawe. (14; 15; 21; 22; 32)

Over 4,500 artifacts and 2,081 historical features were mapped by 2001 and these include petroglyph figures near the summit of the island. The island was declared a National Historical District in 1982.

III.22 **Keoneʻōʻio (La Perouse Bay)**

Village ruins

Keoneʻōʻio means "the sandy place with bonefish" and is the Hawaiian name for La Perouse Bay and its surroundings. It was so named because of the ʻōʻio (bonefish) which frequented the sandy bay bottom and were sweep-netted by fishermen using several canoes at a time.

The first known European ship to anchor at Maui, although no one from it ventured ashore, was commanded by the French captain Jean François de Galaup, Comte de La Perouse, in May of 1786. He noted four small fishing villages in this area and traded with the friendly natives. He noted in his log: "Although the French were the first ... to land on Maui, I did not think it was my right to take possession of it in the name of the King. The customs of Europeans in this respect are completely ridiculous." La Perouse sailed off to what are now known as the French Frigate Shoals, uninhabited western atolls of the Hawaiian

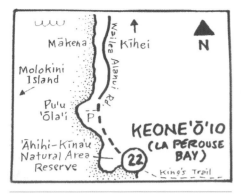

LOCATION: **Seven miles south of Wailea Shopping Village at the end of Mākena Road. One-mile easy hike from the end of a paved road along a cinder trail.**

Islands, and later mysteriously disappeared at sea. It is believed that his two ships were lost in a hurricane off the Solomon Islands. His log with maps survived him and clearly indicated Keoneʻōʻio Bay to be previously much larger than it is today. In 1793, the British explorer Captain Vancouver charted the area and indicated fresh lava flows on either side of the bay, at Cape Kīnaʻu and Cape Hanamanioa. This most recent of Maui's lava flows is dated at about 1790.

Before arriving at Keoneʻōʻio, via the road from Kīhei, one passes through ʻĀhihi-Kīnaʻu Natural Area Reserve, a rugged 2,046 acres of ʻaʻā lava, part of the 1790 flow. Hawaiian village ruins, ancient fishponds, and anchialine ponds can be seen in this reserve. Between Kalaeloa ("the long point") and Kanahena Point is the 40-foot islet Pōhakupaea ("stone that lands [ashore]"). A ban on fishing is strictly enforced in this area.

A legend tells of a couple that lived at Keoneʻōʻio and had two children and some chickens, the latter promised as offerings in sacrifice to Pele. One day an old woman came asking for something to eat and requested a chicken. When told the chickens were already promised, the old woman, who was Pele herself, became furious. She chased the woman and her daughter up the hill, where she covered them in lava, and then chased the man and his son, who almost got away, into the ocean and turned them into stone. Near the source of the 1790 lava flow one can see the form of a petrified woman with her daughter, and offshore the man and his

Paʻalua, a hoʻoulu ua heiau for rain and fish, and Hala Heiau, a hoʻomana shrine for a shark god, are here at Keoneʻōʻio. There are also recent burial sites. Please do not disturb any of the sites or stone features.

son are visible as a larger and a smaller rock poking their heads up from the water. A variation on this story tells of two lovers, Paea and Kalua, who were turned to stone by Pele. He, Po'o Kanaka (Man's Head), stands by the remains of the old fishpond, and she, Pōhaku Paea, resides at Pu'u Na'io ("hill of conquest"), where she was turned into Pu'u Kalualapa, a ridge below the hill.

At Keone'ō'io, numerous rock walls, part of old fishing village ruins, can be seen.

Numerous rock walls, part of old Keone'ō'io fishing village ruins, can be seen. Heiau, hale mua, ko'a, canoe sheds, and dozens of grinding depressions lie close to the shoreline trail in the shade of kiawe trees. No archaeological excavations have taken place here, but other coastal settlements on this part of the island date to around 1100.

Sites such as heiau, hale mua, ko'a, canoe sheds, and dozens of grinding depressions lie close to the shoreline trail in the shade of kiawe trees. Pa'alua, a ho'oulu ua heiau for rain and fish, and Hala Heiau, a ho'omana shrine for a shark god, are here. No archaeological excavations have taken place here, but other coastal settlements on this part of the island date to around 1100. Oral traditions concerning this area link the Big Island chiefs Kauholanuimahu and Ko'i with Keone'ō'io in the 1400s and 1500s. Ko'i settled here, took a wife and raised children. It is also recorded that chief Kalani'ōpu'u landed his war canoes here during a conflict between Maui and Hawai'i in the eighteenth century.

A number of groups are hoping that the entire Keone'ō'io-La Perouse area out to Kanaloa Point will be designated a National Park in the future. A feasibility study has not yet taken place. (15/85; 18/122, 130-133; 21/69; 32/66, 108, 115, 187; 37/222-228; 40)

III.23 **Hoapili Trail**

Trail system

High Chief Hoapili was appointed governor of Maui in 1823, the same year American missionaries arrived in the islands and he converted to Christianity shortly thereafter. As governor he sent criminals convicted of drunkenness, adultery, and other un-Christian-like behavors to hard labor on road construction. The roadways, paved with rough clinkers and cobbles of lava rock gravel, circled around most of the island and linked many small backcountry villages with the more populated areas. Sections of

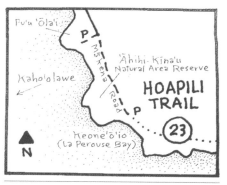

LOCATION: **Seven miles south of Wailea Shopping Village at the end of Mākena Road. One-mile easy hike from the end of a paved road along a coastal trail.**

the trail, designed for horse and foot traffic, can still be seen at Kapalua in Lahaina, Keoneʻōʻio in Makawao, and Waiʻānapanapa in Hāna.

At Keoneʻōʻio, as one approaches Cape Hanamanioa and the western leg of the last Maui (1790) lava flow, ʻaʻā lava rock ruins and the 6-foot-wide Hoapili Trail come into view. This historic roadway was built in the

A portion of the Hoapili Trail is visible again for a stretch at Nu'u in Kaupō.

1840s over the older ala loa ("long road") or King's Trail completed by Kihaapi'ilani in the 16th century. Begun by the great Maui High Chief Pi'ilani, father of Kihaapi'ilani, this rough clinker trail was the original Pi'ilani Highway and even went up into Haleakalā Crater. The newer Hoapili Trail is constructed over this older Kihaapi'ilani Trail and runs for about two miles across the desolate lava field to Kanaio ("the bastard sandalwood tree"), where it regains the coast. The Hoapili Trail then continues another 10 miles through rugged terrain where ancient sites and ahu (cairn or rock piles),

The older ala loa ("long road") or King's Trail, also called Pi'ilani Highway, completed by Kihaapi'ilani in the 1500s, and unlike the 1840s Hoapili Trail, meanders with smooth, water-worn steppingstones as can be seen at Wai'ānapanapa, in Hana.

marking old land divisions and points of long-forgotten significance, can be seen. Curbstones line the pathway so that horses would not be tempted to leave the trail when riders fell asleep on long rides at night.

Where the trail crosses streambeds and gulches, causeways were built by the convicts with only the use of traditional tools and ancient construction techniques. When the missionary Henry T. Cheever traveled on the Hoapili Trail and experienced it first hand shortly after its completion in the late 1840s, he noted "...when considered that it was made by convicts, without sledgehammers, or crowbars, or any other instrument but the human hands, holding a stone, and the Hawaiian Oo, it is worthy of great admiration." (p. 224-5)

Unlike the older Hawaiian trails that often meander and have evenly spaced smooth, water-worn steppingstones as at Wai'ānapanapa, the Hoapili Trail is absolutely straight, perhaps in anticipation of modern freeways. Even though it is straight with little change in elevation, the Hoapili Trail can be a strenuous hike, especially at midday, and should not be attempted without adequate preparation and provisions. (23; 37; 40)

III.24 **Haleakalā**

Volcano crater

(Wikimedia Commons)

The old Hawaiian name for Haleakalā ("house of the sun") was actually Aheleakalā ("rays of the sun" or "snaring [rays] of the sun") because this is where the demigod Māui lassoed the sun and made it slow down on its daily course through the sky. In mythic times the sun moved so quickly through the heavens that Hina, mother of Māui, was unable to dry her kapa cloth in a single day. So one day Māui, the courageous trickster, gathered green coconut at Waiheʻe and made himself a

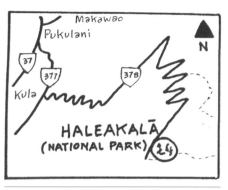

LOCATION: **One-and-a half-hour drive from Kahului Airport, west on Highway 37, 377, and 378.**

coconut fiber rope with 16 snares. Departing from Kekaʻa (see site I.3 and I.4) in West Maui he journeyed to the foot of Haleakalā and climbed to its summit. According to the legend, he waited over-night in a cinder cone called Puʻu O Māui and as the sun rose over the crater's eastern rim at dawn, he caught each of the sun's 16 leg-like rays in his ropes. On the threat of death, the sun agreed that half the year he would travel slowly so there would be long days and the other half he would travel a little faster to make shorter days. From then on the kapa cloth of Hina was able to dry on the long summer days, thanks to Māui catching the sun.

Haleakalā, the largest volcanic crater of its kind in the world, is 21 miles in circumference and 10,023 feet above sea level at its highest point, Puʻu ʻUlaʻula. Seven and a half miles long, the crater is 3,000 feet deep, with two openings in its rim—one at Koʻolau Gap in the northwest, and the other at Kaupō Gap to the southeast. Haleakalā is a typical shield volcano formed over thousands of years of eruptions and lava flows. Later vents spewed lava under high pressure, but lower heat created lava fountains that quickly cooled to form puʻu (cinder cones) on the floor of the crater.

Haleakalā, being and alpine cinder desert with extreme weather conditions, was not a site of year-round residential settlement but it was regularly visited by ancient Hawaiians. Temporary shelter ruins, terraced platforms, stone retaining walls, burial ahu, an ancient paved trail, and numerous cave shelters confirm early visits to the "House of the Sun." Some of the stone platforms are believed to be heiau and can be found on top of or inside puʻu. Little remains to be seen of these religious structures where Lilinoe, the goddess of mists at Haleakalā, was worshipped. Such a heiau site was on the highest summit of the mountain, called Puʻuʻulaʻula ("Red Hill"). It was destroyed when the park overlook was built. The only sign of ancient structures remaining near the summit are the low rock wall enclosures that were possibly kahu (guardian) shelters. The small, circular shelters may be seen beside the trailhead to Sliding Sands, at the southern base of Pā Kaʻoao ("White Hill").

Some 60 stone platforms and terraces, 10 open stone shelters, several hundred ahu, and a section of ancient paved trail have been surveyed within the crater. The trail, which is 6 to 8 feet wide in places, was one of High Chief Kihaapiʻilani's construction projects and made it possible to travel across East Maui without using the usual coastal trails. North of Kāwilinau ("the Bottomless Pit"), this ancient road cannot be reached by a maintained trail. The park service asks that all hikers remain on marked trails.

Haleakalā was not a site of year-round residential settlement but was regularly visited by ancient Hawaiians. Temporary shelter ruins, terraced platforms, stone retaining walls, burial ahu, an ancient paved trail, and numerous cave shelters confirm early visits to the "House of the Sun." This is one such temporary shelter.

Keahuamanono Heiau was built by Kaoao, younger brother of Kekaulike, on the summit of Haleakalā Peak, above Kapalaoa Cabin, at an elevation of 8,201 feet. It is a rectangular rock wall enclosure, measuring 56 by 30 feet and as tall as 18 feet in places.

Besides accessing the gods in this high altitude location and providing an alternate travel route across the island, Haleakalā was also a place of industry. There were numerous adze production sites on the western rim of the crater where quality basalt was procured and roughedout for adze hammer tools. Basalt adze hammer-stones, rejects and flakes, were found and dated to between 1250 and 1700s.

Sites that are easily accessible to hikers inside the crater are Ana ma Kauahi, Nā Piko Haua, and Hōlua Caves. Ana ma Kauahi is a small shelter about one quarter mile north of Kapalaoa ("the whale") Cabin, along the right side of the trail leading to Puʻu Naue ("trembling hill") and Hōlua (sled). This shelter cave is only about 5 feet deep and 10

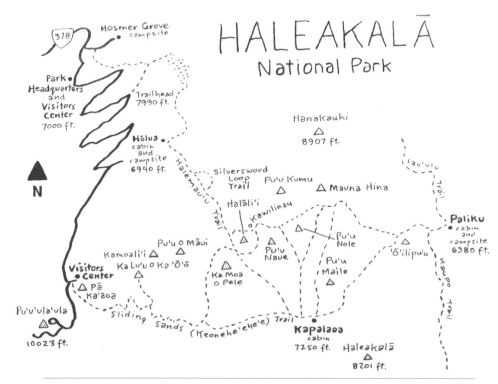

Easiest access to the crater is at Sliding Sands Trail near the summit or by Halemau'u Trail at a slightly lower elevation. Kaupō Trail is the only approach from the Hāna district, a steep and strenuous 8.5-mile hike. There are three cabins with campgrounds in the crater. Permits are required.

feet in diameter. It is entered from above. Nā Piko Haua ("Long Cave") is a lava tube about a quarter mile south of Hōlua Cabin. A side trail leads to the cave entrance, which is accessed by a steep metal ladder. Flashlights are necessary for exploring this jagged 'a'ā lava tube that stretches several hundred feet in a southerly direction. Umbilical cord stumps of babies from the Kaupō district were wrapped in kapa cloth and mother's hair, and were placed in this cave to collect mana for the child. Hōlua Cave is just behind and above the national park cabin of the same name at about the 7,000-foot elevation. The cave was probably used as a shelter and lookout by early Hawaiians, and it has been carbon dated to 700–900. Hōlua is a narrow, but level, 25-foot tunnel into the crater ridge.

The 27,284-acre crater is part of the Haleakalā National Park. The park service maintains campgrounds and cabins within the crater, for which permits are required. Short hikes into the crater are possible without a permit, but, due to the sudden changes in high-elevation weather, it is advisable to check with rangers on prevailing conditions. It is also essential to familiarize oneself beforehand with the park's regulations for minimum impact on the fragile environment. It is im-

The 27,284-acre crater is part of the Haleakalā National Park. The best views of the crater can be found at Leleiwi ("bone altar") Overlook, Kalahaku ("proclaim the lord"), Pā Ka'oao ("White Hill"), and Pu'u 'Ula'ula ("Red Hill").

portant to be aware of how one can best protect the unique and delicate ecosystem of Haleakalā. As with all archaeological sites, those within the crater are irreplaceable cultural treasures. Please protect them by not walking on or climbing them and not altering them in any way. Approach all sites within the park with respect.

Half of Haleakalā is in the district of Makawao and half lies in the Hāna district. Easiest access to the crater is from Makawao district, either by Sliding Sands Trail or by Halemau'u Trail. Also, the best views of the crater are afforded from overlooks at Leleiwi ("bone altar"), Kalahaku ("proclaim the lord"), Pā Ka'oao ("White Hill"), and Pu'u 'Ula'ula ("Red Hill") all of which are in the Makawao district. Kaupō Trail is the only approach from the Hāna district, a steep and strenuous 8.5-mile hike.

For information contact: Haleakalā National Park, P.O. Box 369, Makawao, HI 96768; (808) 572-4400; www.nps.gov/hale. There is an entrance fee to the national park and permits are required for camping and sunrise summit visits. (8/235-259; 23; 27; 37/259-267; 40/ 293)

> *Akāka wale 'o Haleakalā.*
> Haleakalā stands in full view.
> [Said of anything that is very obvious or clearly understood.] (28/13)
> —Hawaiian saying

IV. **East Maui: Hāna**

Hāna means "alert." It is not a bad disposition to be alert while exploring this laid-back region of East Maui. There is much to see in this area, which is clearly one of the few remaining places in the Islands where the quality of old Hawai'i is still apparent. From the hot and arid kua 'āina (backside) of Kahikinui on the south side of Haleakalā, through Kaupō and Hāna to the lush and wet Ko'olau region in the north, the Hāna district is special both in its nature and in its culture. In many ways Hāna is ancient Maui.

At Nu'u, on Maui's southeast coast, 30 carved petroglyphs and 75 painted pictograms depict human and animal figures. This dancing human figure is engraved into the rock surface but there are also pictograms that were painted.

On the drier side of the Hāna land section, in Kahikinui ("great Tahiti"), there are many archaeological sites that are not yet open to the public. However, in the adjacent ahupua'a of Kaupō, 84 acres of the Nu'u region were acquired by the Hawaiian Island Land Trust. This area is now accessible to the public with its cultural sites.

Further to the east, below the great Kaupō ("night landing") Gap, are many ancient sites such as Lo'alo'a ("pitted") Heiau, a sixteenth-century multiterraced temple foundation attributed to Kekaulike and re-dedicated by Liholiho, son of Kamehameha I, when he was still a child in 1800. Hale o Kāne Heiau, further up Kaupō Trail and west of Manawainui ("large water branch") Stream, and Pōpōiwi Heiau, also known as Kealalaua'e, on the hill above Mokulau ("many islets") are also in this area. Pōpōiwi was dedicated by Kekaulike about 1730, and was a pu'uhonua, measuring 168 feet by 330 feet, with a 20-foot-high terraced wall on its seaward side. These sites are mentioned only in passing for the heiau are on private property and as of this writing inaccessible. Huialoha ("meeting [of] compassion") Church, overlooking

At the mouth of Hāna Harbor, just off Kauʻiki Head, is a 1.5-acre islet called Puʻukiʻi ("image hill"). It was once reached by a footbridge and a small lighthouse is on the little island's 72-foot summit.

the ancient surfing spot at Mokulau Peninsula, is an early historic ruin, which was originally built in 1859 of rock and lime plaster.

On the far eastern end of the island is the village of Hāna. One of the most notorious ancient aliʻi was the high chief Hua, of Hāna. He had the very wise kahuna Luahoʻomoe as his advisor, but, not wishing to take Luahoʻomoe's council, Hua slew him, and, as a consequence, the chief and his people suffered dearly. A drought came upon the land and, everywhere that Hua or his people traveled to escape the devastation, the drought followed. Three years later, Hua died of thirst and starvation on the island of Hawaiʻi. Still the drought continued. The two sons of Luahoʻomoe had been warned by their father before his death to hide in the mountains and await a sign. The great kahuna Naula a Maikea of Oʻahu realized the cause of the drought and looked for a solution. He saw that over the island of Maui there was a small cloud, and he knew that the sons of Luahoʻomoe, Kaʻakakai and Kaʻanahua, were still alive and held the promise for future rain. Naula quickly traveled to Maui. His arrival was the needed sign and, together with the two brothers, he made the acceptable offering to Lono that finally ended the drought. Kaʻakakai and Kaʻanahua returned to Hāna, where they served the people of East Maui with the wisdom passed on to them by their father.

Because of its isolation, East Maui was often ruled separately from West Maui in ancient times. The Hāna coast was even dominated at various times by Hawaiian chiefs who invaded from the Kohala coast of the Big Island, 30 miles across the 'Alenuihāhā Channel. Kamehameha the Great of Hawai'i Island succeeded in capturing Hāna and all of West Maui, as he fought to unite the Hawaiian Islands under his rule. Ka'uiki Hill in Hāna was the site of numerous struggles between the armies of Hawai'i and those of Maui. Queen Ka'ahumanu, the favorite wife of Kamehameha the Great, was born here amidst one of the ongoing conflicts. Mythological struggle occurred among the gods at Ka Iwi o Pele in Hāna, where the volcano goddess Pele is said to have been defeated in battles with both her older sister and the pig god, Kamapua'a.

The largest heiau in the state is located along the Hāna coast, and many other natural and archaeological features can be found at Wai'ānapanapa State Park, as well as at 'Ohe'o in the coastal region of Kīpahulu. As one rounds East Maui, the natural beauty and traditional agricultural setting of Ke'anae is clearly another distinctive wahi pana on the north shore of the Hāna land section. (3; 4/30; 6/ 92; 17; 20; 21; 22; 23; 27; 20; 36; 37; 40/333-347; 41; 43)

> *'Oi'oi 'o Maui Hikina.*
> East Maui forges ahead.
> [Those of East Maui are said to be very active and able to withstand anything.] (37/261)
> —Hawaiian saying

Hāna (East Maui) District Map

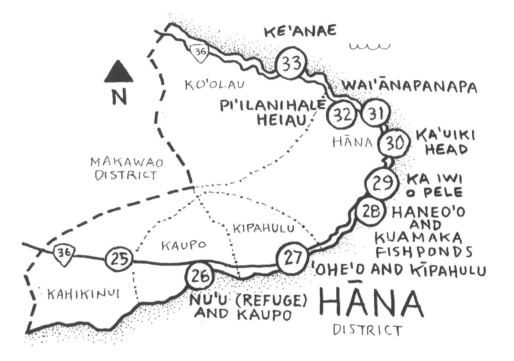

IV.25 **Kahikinui**

Natural and archaeological features

Kahikinui means "the Great Ta-hiti," and Native Hawaiian historian Samuel Kamakau related how Kāne and Kanaloa, two of the major Hawaiian gods, after a stop on Kahoʻolawe visited Kahihkinui, where they established the fishpond of Kanaloa at Lualaʻilua in western Kahikinui. Traditional chants also inform us of Laamaikahiki, the son of a renowned voyaging chief from Tahiti, who came to Kahikinui via Kauaʻi but left for Kahoʻolawe because it was

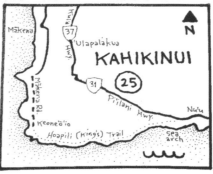

LOCATION: **Viewed from Piʻilani Highway, 31, between 4 and 10 miles from Ulapalakua.**

too windy in this part of Maui. From Kahoʻolawe Laamaikahiki journeyed back to his father's homeland along the stretch of ocean called Ke Ala i Kahiki, "the Road to Tahiti."

Kahikinui, a windswept and seemingly desolate region, is one of the twelve moku of Maui Island and part of the Hana District. Bounded by the relentlessly rough ʻAlanuihāhā Channel and the high mountain ridge (9,700-foot elevation) of Haleakalā, Kahikinui offers a view of the Kohala coast of Hawai'i Island on a clear day. The eastern and western boundaries of Kahikinui have shifted over the years and have settled at Manawainui Gulch in the east and Auwahi in the west. It is dry land that receives its rain not from the prevailing tradewinds but from intermittent kona weather and upcountry fog-drip precipitation. In ancient times this kua 'āina or "backside" of the island was actually well populated and settled by small farming and fishing communities, more so in the western part of the moku than in the soil-poor eastern section.

Extensive surveys of the region have uncovered more than 3,000 archaeological features, including heiau (56 have been identified with over 100 likely in the entire moku), house sites, agricultural terraces, burials, irrigation dams, wells, petroglyphs, trails, a kahua platform, a hōlua sled ramp, and other unique features. The first settlement pattern map drawn up by archaeologists in Hawai'i was done of Kahikinui. According to radiocarbon dates early visitors to Kahikinui arrived around 1000 AD but likely did not really settle in the area until the 1400s. By the 1500s the population had doubled and by the 1700s it had doubled again.

On May 29, 1786, Admiral Jean-François de La Perouse joyfully observed the villages of Kahikinui and wrote in his log: "The island of Mowhee looked delightful." He was the first to map this stretch of the island but due to the rough coastline he did not put ashore. In March of 1793, Captain George Vancouver described the same lands as having "... no indications of being inhabited and were almost destitute of vegetable production."

Following Kamehameha the Great's conquest of Maui in the late 18th century, his dynasty quickly divided up the lands. When the Great Mahele of 1848 legalized the ownership of private property Kahikinui was divided between two heirs of Kamehameha, grandchildren Prince Lot, who would later become Kamehameha V, and Princess Ruth Ke'elikōlani. Lot apparently did not like the land award and traded it to the Hawaiian Kingdom for something more to his liking. Today Lot's portion of Kahikinui is held by the Department of Hawaiian Homelands of the State of Hawai'i and should not be trespassed without permission. In fact, none of the archaeological sites mentioned here are accessible at this time, but as one drives along Pi'ilani Highway, know that this rocky coastal landscape and high mountain slope, are a culturally significant place. From the fisher folk and sweet potato farmers to the cattle ranchers and homesteaders, Kahikinui itself is a time capsule of the past yet to be fully opened.

A curious site near Luala'ilua (also not accessible) is the petroglyph footprints said to be step marks left behind by Menehune as they carried heavy rocks at night to build Lo'alo'a Heiau in Kaupō, 15 miles away. Another explanation is that they are the footprints of people caught in a hardening flow of smooth pahoehoe lava. But clearly they are carved ki'i pōhaku, petroglyphs. The "footprints" which range in size from four to ten inches point in various directions over a 35-foot area and are anywhere from three to six inches apart. Most of the foot pictures look like those of children because of their small size. It is not known why these etched footprints were carved in stone at this place.

Various legends are set around these Luala'ilua Hills in western Kahikinui; for instance there is the tale of a man-eating creature that preyed on innocent travelers who unwittingly came this way. Eventually, the daughter of one of the creature's victims tricked the monster and cast it to its death into the crater.

An historic ruin that one may glimpse in passing along the highway is the Saint Ynez Church built by a Kahikinui native and Catholic convert named Simeon Kaoao. Constructed in the 1830s on the rise of Pu'u Ānuenue (Hill of the Rainbow), just along the highway on a former heiau site (as many of the Christian churches were in Hawai'i), all that remains today is a low basalt rock wall held together with lime and coral mortar. The destroyed roof has been replaced by a temporary plywood structure thanks to Ka 'Ohana o Kahikinui, "The Family of Kahikinui," who are actively resettling the area. However, this is not a tourist stop, so please do not trespass.

Nevertheless, an interesting event occurred here at Saint Ynez. Two faithful Catholic men were arrested for praying with some of the local women and were tied together in the infamous pa'a kaula, "tying with ropes." In 1837 King Kamehameha III outlawed the Catholic religion and a judge in Wailuku was determined to bring the offending catechists in Kahikinui to justice. The two native Hawaiian churchmen were marched the long way around the island, a journey that covered about 90 miles over the course of a month. In every village they passed through sympathizers joined their ranks and followed them to Wailuku. The two devout offenders were released upon arrival at court, as the accompanying crowd was apparently too much for officials to deal with. So much for the "tying with ropes." The Catholic mission was finally granted legitimacy in 1846. Just past the chapel, on the mauka side of the road an unnamed heiau can be seen.

The pānānā or "sighting wall" is a remarkable architectural feature, 24-feet long and 6-feet tall, aligned to the stars of the Southern Cross as a celestial navigation compass pointing towards Kahikinui, the Great Tahiti.

Another fascinating site in Kahikinui is the pānānā, or compass wall, an 'a'ā rock structure 24-feet long, running east-west, parallel to the ocean, and standing 6-feet tall with a notch in its middle (like the achet of an Egyptian pylon temple). Archaeologist Patrick Kirch describes it as follows: "About 50 meters seaward of the [pānānā] wall there is a stone cairn, an ahu, constructed in the same precise masonry style as the wall itself and, a short distance away, a pāhoehoe upright slab. These two features are framed by the sides of the notch when one stands slightly inland of the wall. In the fifteenth century AD, these features would have bracketed the position of the Southern Cross when the main axis of the cross was at its vertical position. In fact, the perpendicular azimuth of the wall, as viewed through the notch, is within one degree of the orientation of the Southern Cross when its kite shape is at its most upright. The Hawaiians called the Southern Cross Hōkūke'a and knew that it pointed the way back to Kahiki." The pānānā or "sighting wall" is a remarkable architectural feature aligned here in Kahikinui as a celestial navigation compass pointing back to the Great Tahiti.

Keep your eyes open for the natural and archaeological sites as you drive through Kahikinui but do not stop on the highway and please do not trespass the sites. (3; 15; 17; 20; 22; 23; 27; 32; 37; 40)

IV.26 **Nuʻu Landing and Kaupō**

Natural and archaeological features

There is the story of a fisherman who lived with his wife in Kahikinui, just west of Kaupō, where he cared for a small coastal fishpond. One day when the fisherman was away two strangers came to their hale and asked for some fish. The wife replied that her husband was not at home and that they could have some fish when he returned. The strangers, who happened to be the gods Kāne and Kanaloa (some renderings say they were Kū and Hina), stormed off angry at this answer and went to the fishpond, which

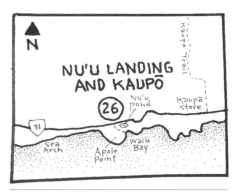

LOCATION: Nu'u Refuge is 35 miles from Kahului, on Pi'ilani Hwy, Route 31. A HILT sign-posted gate is near mile marker 31. Park on the grass.

they promptly destroyed with their supernatural powers. When the fisherman returned he inquired of his wife what terrible thing had happened to the pond and she told him of the two strangers who had just left, going toward Kaupō. The fisherman followed the destructive pair to Nu'u but they had gone on to Kaupō and were now heading up the steep trail to Haleakalā Crater. The fisherman continued his pursuit, meeting a female relative of his and asking her if she had seen the two men. She replied that these were not men but gods and he had best not go after them if he wished to live a long life. Right then lightning struck, thunder rolled and an earthquake rumbled as Kāne and Kanaloa cleared a pathway for themselves into the crater by creating Kaupō Gap. The fisherman wisely decided it was time to go home.

The great Kaupō ("night landing") Gap is actually an expansive fan-shaped outpouring of futile soil created by a late lava flow from Haleakalā Crater. This, together with the right amount of rainfall, was why this area was so productive in sweet potato cultivation. The trailhead that leads up through the Gap and into the crater is not far from Kaupō General Store on Pi'ilani Highway, the only store for miles around. The trail goes through Kaupō Ranch land but access along the trail is granted to hikers in and out of the national park.

Archaeologist Winslow Walker, who did a first general survey of Maui in the late 1920s, described the ruins of several ritual sites in Kaupō. Papakea Heiau, a walled structure had a large paved court with two higher terraces. There was Ka'ili'ili Heiau with walls 6 feet thick and 5 feet high, filled with a'a pebbles and coral bits. Halekou Heiau had an open platform and was surrounded by many house sites, walls, and grave platforms. But the most important temples in Kaupō were Lo'alo'a and Pōpōiwi, dedicated in the 1730s by High Chief Kekaulike of Maui. Covering an area of more than 12,000 square feet Lo'alo'a ("pitted") Heiau was a multi-terraced luakini heiau, a place of ritual human sacrifice.

It is oriented to the northeast and the star cluster Makali'i ("little eyes"), which when appearing indicated the beginning of the Makahiki festival, a time of peace and tribute collection. Pōpōiwi Heiau, also known as Kānemalohemo, on the hill above Mokulau ("many islets"), was according to one source dedicated as a pu'uhonua, a place of refuge. Covering 3.5 acres and measuring 168-feet by 330-feet, with a 20-foot-high terraced wall on its seaward side, it is an impressive ancient structure. Its bow-like corner wall points directly toward the Kohala coast of Hawai'i Island. These two heiau were built at a time when Kekaulike shifted his powerbase to Kaupō in order to better challenge his constant rivals across the 'Alanuihāhā Channel. Liholiho, the son of Kamehameha the Great, rededicated Lo'alo'a Heiau in 1800, when he was still a child. There is also a Hale o Kāne Heiau, farther up Kaupō Trail but all of these sites are on Kaupō Ranch land and require permission to visit. These heiau sites are inaccessible as of this writing and are mentioned only in passing for they are part of the rich history of this 'āina.

The accessible sites in Kaupō are found at Nu'u Landing, a former historic cattle loading point for the 19th and early 20th century ranching in the area. But there are also ancient cultural sites in this wahi pana.

Nu'u means "heights" and that is certainly what one sees as one looks mauka, toward the mountains. Haleakalā Crater towers above the landscape with a visible ridgeline close to 10,000 feet in elevation. Nu'u is the

At Nu'u, on Maui's southeast coast, 30 carved petroglyphs and 75 painted pictograms depict human and turtle figures, as seen here. Dog images are also present on the basalt cliff near the bay. The pictograms were painted with pigments made from red alaea earth, sometimes mixed with kukui nut juice and ulu, breadfruit sap.

name of the ahupua'a, or smaller land division, within Kaupō moku and is the name of the bay. Nu'u is also thought to be the name of a cliff-dwelling god of these parts.

In 2011 the Hawaiian Islands Land Trust, with funding from the Hawaii Department of Land and Natural Resources, the U.S. Fish and Wildlife Service, and private doners, secured ownership of 82 acres of coastal land from Kaupō Ranch. The $4-million acquisition was desig-

The famous springwater of Waiu, at the base of Pu'u Mane'one'o, is here at Nu'u. There are also springs that feed the Salt Pond at Nu'u as seen here.

nated a refuge, conservation area, and native habitat with shoreline access for recreation, cultural activities, and archaeological preservation.

Within the Nu'u Refuge, between the highway and the beach, some 30 petroglyphs and 75 painted pictograms can be found. They include animal and human figures in basic early Hawaiian style. The pictograms were painted with pigments made from red alaea earth, sometimes mixed with kukui nut juice and ulu, breadfruit sap. There are also house sites, heiau, fishing shrines, a canoe landing, and a section of the Hoapili Trail running through the area. The so-called Salt Pond of Nu'u is actually a springfed brackish wetland for native birds with a sacred wellspring. The famous springwater of Waiu is also here at Nu'u, at the base of Pu'u Mane'one'o.

A thriving ancient fishing village was located here at Nu'u, but its population began to dwindle in the mid-1800s due to illness and as the area was leased for ranching. A pier was constructed in the late 1800s for its deep natural harbor and its usefulness in cattle loading. The pier was later abandoned, but its foundations can still be seen. Only five houses were still occupied in the 1920s when Walker did his archaeological survey. Today Nu'u is uninhabited.

However, while sailing past Kaupō in 1786, Admiral Jean-François de La Perouse described the landscape as populated with small farms and productive fields. In fact Kaupō was a very rich agricultural area in the 16th through the 18th centuries, particularly in u'ala, sweet potato. It was partly for this reason that the Hawai'i Island warriors of Kalani'opu'u, who held the hill fort of Ka'uiki in Hānā, pushed into Kaupō and brutally attacked the farmers here—they wanted the food supply. The battle was called Ke Kaua o Ka Lae Hohoa, "the foreheads beaten with clubs," because of the way the innocent farmers and villagers were dispatched. When Kahekili, ruling chief of Maui, heard of the slaughter he sent his forces to avenge the loss of his people. The two opposing armies clashed at Pu'u Mane'one'o and the Hawaiian warriors of Kalani'opu'u were eventually routed, fleeing in their canoes. The earlier massacre of civilians has usually only been noted in passing by histo-

A thriving ancient fishing village was located here at Nu'u, but its population began to dwindle in the mid-1800s due to illness and ranching moving in. This little cove served as one of the few canoe landing along this rough coastline.

rians, who generally focus instead on the role of Kamehameha I in the subsequent fight. In his first major skirmish, the young warrior-chief saved the life of his mentor, the expert warrior Kekuhaupi'o, who had become tangled in u'ala vines. Because of his heroic actions, Kamehameha received the name Pai'ea, "hard-shelled crab." A year later, in 1776, Kalani'opu'u brought his fight back to Maui landing at Keone'o'io (site III.22) with his double-hulled war canoes reaching as far as Honua'ula (site III.20). His warriors proceeded to ravage the land and its people as they forced their way to Wailuku in two waves (site II.12), both times being devastated by Kahekili's armies. Kalani'opu'u survived this campaign and returned several more times to fight on Maui, with two further conflicts at Kaupō.

A detailed survey of the Nu'u Refuge is currently underway in hopes that it will help The Hawaiian Islands Land Trust (HILT) with its plans for historic preservation and protection of cultural sites. Habitat restoration for endangered bird species including the ae'o (Hawaiian stilt) and the 'alae ke'oke'o (Hawaiian coot) and educational outreach are also important parts of HILTs mission. Volunteer opportunities and occasional free, guided tours are offered of the area. Contact: HILT, P.O. Box 965, 2371 W. Vineyard Street, Wailuku, HI 96793. (808) 244-5263, info@hilt. org. Pōhaku Cultural Tours also offers excursions for a fee (PCT, P.O. Box 865, Makawao, HI 96768. info@pohakuculturaltours.com).

Huialoha ("meeting [of] compassion") Church, overlooking the ancient surfing spot at Mokulau Peninsula, is an early historic site, which was built in 1859 of rock and lime plaster when there was a strong Hawaiian congregation in the area. When Kahikinui (site VI.25) was abandoned in the mid-1800s many of the residents moved to Kaupō. (4; 6; 8; 15; 22; 23; 27; 37; 40)

V.27 'Ohe'o and Kīpahulu

Natural and archaeological features

Kīpahulu is the moku or land section, adjacent to Kaupō, that includes 'Ohe'o ("something special") Gulch. Incorrectly referred to as Seven Sacred Pools, 'Ohe'o, actually has many more pools than seven, depending on the water level at any given time, and may have no other traditional claim to being sacred other than the fact that the pools were kapu to menstruating women. Nevertheless, the 'Ohe'o area is clearly sacred in terms of its natural beauty and elemental enchantment. The power of this wahi pana ("celebrated place") is obvious to all who visit.

There is a story that relates the number seven to the pools as one ascends from the salty sea-fed pools to the brackish waters of the lower pools at Kēloa ("long waiting") Point, then on to the fresh, clearer waters of the upper pools. It was said that people were brought here for the purpose of winning them back to "the ways of goodness" by making a spiritual ascent from one pool to the next. The first pool was called 'Akahi, and symbolized inexperience. The second pool, Luakapu, related to the lifting of restrictions. The third pool was 'Ekolu, and had to do with the road to perfection. The fourth pool, 'Eha'eha, being the middle of the ascent, symbolized the longing for perfection, and the fifth pool, above the bridge, called Laulima, was the removal of error through reverence. The

However, it was in the immediate neighborhood of the pools that Pele, the volcano goddess, was said to have pursued Kamapua'a, the pig god. The chase

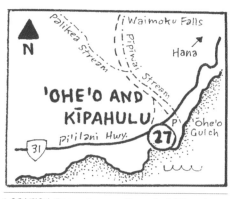

LOCATION: **Ten miles southwest of Hāna town along Pi'ilani Highway (Route 31), mile marker 42; seven miles from Kaupō. Haleakalā National Park: (808) 248-8251 or 248-7375. There is a $10 parking fee per vehicle. Walkins, bicyclists and motorcyclists pay $5.**

culminated at Kīpahulu Valley, with Kamapua'a diving into a stream, now known as Pua'alu'u ("diving pig"). He surfaced in Pepeiaolepo

Some of the 700 archaeological features in the National Park at Kīpahulu include house site foundations as the one pictured here.

Two miles up the maintained trail from Pi'ilani Highway is Waimoku ("flash flood") Falls, with a 400-foot cascade.

("dirty ear") Bay at the mouth of the stream, with his ears full of mud. It was possible for the demigod Kamapua'a to turn into a man, a pig, the white shoot of the hina tree, or a reef triggerfish known in Hawaiian as the humuhumunukunukuāpua'a.

Palikea ("white cliff") is the mainstream entering 'Ohe'o Gulch. Its source is at Haleakalā, over the 6,000-foot elevation, and it flows the entire length of Kīpahulu Valley. Pīpīwai ("sprinkling water") Stream is a tributary of the longer stream and boasts two spectacular waterfalls. Makahiku Falls, a half-mile hike from Pi'ilani Highway, is 184 feet high. A mile and a half further upstream is Waimoku ("flash flood") Falls, with a 400-foot cascade. Trails to these spots are maintained by the National Park Service, as 'Ohe'o Gulch and Kīpahulu Valley were designated a part of Haleakalā National Park in 1969. Near Waimoku Falls along Pīpīwai Trail are some petroglyphs but the park service does not direct visitors to them. Beyond the falls in upper Kīpahulu Valley is a Scientific Research Reserve, which is closed to the public. Its steep cliffs and rugged terrain help keep it inaccessible, protecting its rare birds and endemic vegetation, some of which are found nowhere else in the world. Hawaiians considered this valley the home of Laka, a god worshipped by canoe builders, probably because of the quality of koa wood gathered from here for canoes. Kīpahulu means "fetch (from) exhausted gardens."

Below the highway are a park ranger station, visitor center and the start of a half-mile loop trail that takes one down to a view of Kūloa Point and Pepeiaolepo Bay. From here the island of Hawai'i can be seen on a clear day, 30-miles away. Kīpahulu was a fairly populated area in former times and over 700 features have been surveyed on parklands. Stabilized house sites and other ancient ruins such as fishing shrines, heiau, canoe ramps, and old taro patches, can be seen all along the coastal area. Not far from the park headquarters is Kanekoela Heiau, third largest in the State, and a place where kāhuna were apparently trained in their profession. It is planned that in the future this temple will be restored and opened to the public, and it has recently been added to the Haleakalā National Park. Other heiau in the area were Poʻomanini ("manini fish head"), a heiau that stood beside Puaʻaluʻu Stream, and Wailoa

Not far from the visitor center at the Haleakalā National Park in Kīpahulu is a reconstructed house typical of ancient Hawaiʻi.

("long water") Heiau, 50 yards above the road beside ʻOheʻo Gulch. These latter two sites are now destroyed. (4; 16; 20; 32; 37/159)

> *Ka makani kāʻili aloha o Kīpahulu.*
> The love-snatching wind of Kīpahulu.
> [A woman of Kīpahulu, Maui, listened to the entreaties of a man from Oʻahu and left her husband and children to go with him to his home island. Her husband missed her very much and grieved. He mentioned his grief to a kahuna skilled in hana aloha (love) sorcery, who told the man to find a container with a lid. The man was told to talk into it, telling of his love for his wife. Then the kahuna uttered an incantation into the container, closed it, and hurled it into the sea. The wife was fishing one morning at Kālia, Oʻahu, when she saw a container floating in on a wave. She picked it up and opened it, whereupon a great longing possessed her to go home. She walked until she found a canoe to take her to Maui.] (31/158)
> —Hawaiian saying

V.28 **Haneoʻo and Kuamaka Fishponds**

Coastal fishponds

Just to the south of Kōkī Beach Park are two privately owned fishponds, reputedly built by the fish god, Kūʻula, grandson of the great Hāna kahuna, Luahoʻome. Kūʻula and his wife, Hinapukuia, lived at Hāna with their three children, the most celebrated being their son, ʻAiʻai. Kūʻula always had plenty of fish in his ponds and always shared what he had with his neighbors. However, large numbers of fish were suddenly missing from his pond and he discovered that this was

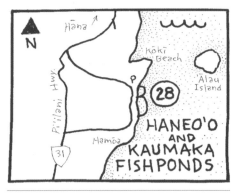

LOCATION: **Two miles south of Hāna town off Piʻilani Highway (31), on Haneoʻo Loop Road left at the Hāmoa turn-off.**

due to Koʻone, the eel-man from Molokaʻi, who started visiting the pond by night in order to feed on the easy catch. ʻAiʻai caught the great eel with a magic hook given to him by his father and smashed the eel's jaw on shore, where it can still be seen as a lava rock formation. Its body can also be seen in the coastal lava (the same image described above as the enchanted eel-chief from Molokaʻi). When worshippers of the great eel from Molokaʻi took revenge on Kūʻula's family by burning their house, the spirits of Kūʻula and his wife left their bodies to dwell with the fish in the sea. ʻAiʻai received all his father's skill and he taught the people of

Hāna how to make fish line, nets and lures. The first ko'a (fishing shrine) dedicated to Kū'ula was said to have been built here by 'Ai'ai. After a time 'Ai'ai moved to Kīpahulu teaching the arts of fish husbandry and the protocol for receiving Kū'ula's blessings. He proceeded on to Kaupō and then around Maui, teaching and establishing ko'a as he went. Fishing shrines became more numerous than heiau as 'Ai'ai traveled throughout the Hawaiian Islands.

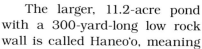

'Ālau Islet lies just offshore from Haneo'o Fishpond. Please be respectful of sites and do not trespass.

The larger, 11.2-acre pond with a 300-yard-long low rock wall is called Haneo'o, meaning the "mature soul," and was reportedly rebuilt in 1808 by Kamehameha the Great. According to tradition, this pond and the small neighboring one are much older but the original construction date is not known. The rock walls were at one time 20 to 25 feet wide and 3 feet higher than they now stand but were damaged in a 1946 tsunami.

Lobsters were so abundant at Haneo'o pond that they would crawl up the wall at night and could be easily harvested by torchlight from the top of the causeway. There is a six-foot-wide mākāhā at the center of the pond wall to let fish in at high tides. When the current changes the sluice gate is closed in order to retain the catch.

A female mo'o (lizard) named Kihawahine is reputed to live here at Haneo'o and also at Moku'ula Fishpond in Lahaina (site I.7). This particular deity was highly revered by both commoners and ali'i in ancient times. In fact, Kihawahine was the 'aumakua (ancestral guardian spirit) of the ali'i Pi'ilani lineage and carried tremendous mana even for Kamehameha the Great who revered her as the goddess "land holders" and placed her on an equal kapu status with Kuka'ilimoku, "the land grabber." Over the years, on several occasions, it is said that she has been seen by local residents.

Kuamaka is the smaller fishpond and is maintained by Hāna community groups. It is also called Loko Iki or "small pond." The ponds are owned and maintained by several families and should not be trespassed. In the 1970s, out of town fishermen regularly came to the ponds and overfished them to sell the catch to West Maui restaurants. A traditional kapu has since been placed on the ponds in order to maintain a healthy and sustainable pond system. The fishponds can be viewed from the road but are accessed only with special permission. (16; 32; 37; 40; 41)

V.29 **Ka Iwi O Pele**

Volcanic cinder hill

Ka Iwi O Pele, which means "bones of Pele," is the legendary location of a battle that the volcano goddess Pele fought with her older sister, Nāmakaokahaʻi, goddess of the ocean. It is said that Pele's bones were stripped of their flesh and buried here as a memorial to her defeat, but her spirit rose up and went to Kīlauea on the Big Island.

A young Molokaʻi chief visiting Hāna for a surfing contest once scoffed at the suggestion that the cinder hill was sacred to Pele, and, as soon as he uttered

LOCATION: Two miles south of Hāna town on Piʻilani Highway (31), left at the Hāmoa turn-off. Easily viewed from the highway.

his disrespectful words, he was changed into a large eel. A deep track, 30 feet long in pāhoehoe lava was left where the enchanted chief slithered away into the sea.

It was also here that Pele was ravished by her constant adversary, Kamapuaʻa, the pig god. Clearly, this was not a lucky spot for the volcano goddess. It is also said that the mythological figure, Lonomuku, left the earth from the top of this red cinder hill to go live on the moon. Another tradition speaks of Māui pulling up the Hawaiian Islands at Ka Iwi O Pele with his magic fishhook Manaiakalani ("made fast to the heavens") baited with an ʻalae bird. A chant also states that the hook stuck at Kaʻuiki Head.

From Ka Iwi O Pele one can see a small offshore island, 'Ālau, said to have been created by Pele. Its name means "many rocks," and it is set aside as a bird sanctuary. Less than a half mile from the beach, 'Ālau is accented with several coconut palms on its 150-foot summit. A good view of the islet is afforded from Kōkī Beach Park on the south side of Ka Iwi O Pele.

Mauka (mountainside) of Ka Iwi O Pele, on private land, is the agricultural temple Hale O Lono Heiau, measuring 100-feet square and recently dated to 1400–1650. Kaluanui Heiau (c. 1650–1820), thought to be a shrine for kapa beating, is also in the Hāmoa area and, together with Hale O Lono, was surveyed in 1993.

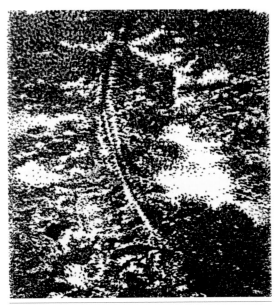

The petrified form of Laumeki, the eel, with its gaping mounth is on private property but can be viewed by taking the horseback ride to Leho'ula Beach, arranged at Hotel Hāna-Maui. Laumeki of Moloka'i left an imprint of his eel-body in the lava rock shoreline when he was slain below Ka Iwi O Pele.

Ka Iwi O Pele can be viewed easily from Pi'ilani Highway (Route 31) and should not be trespassed as it is private property. A 105-acre parcel of Ka Iwi O Pele is owned by Oprah Winfrey. The petrified form of Laumeki, the eel, can be viewed by taking the horseback ride to Leho'ula Beach, arranged through Hotel Hāna-Maui. (4/ 26; 17/61; 32/ 71, 41, 11; 37/141-144; 40)

> *Lewa ka waha o ka puhi o Laumeki.*
> The mouth of the eel of Laumeki gapes.
> [Said of one who talks so much that his mouth is hardly ever closed. Laumeki was an eel-man who lived at Wailau, Moloka'i. When he saw that Kū'ula's fishpond at Hāna, Maui, was always full of fish, he decided to assume his eel form and go there to steal some. On one of his thieving expeditions, he was caught by a magic hook and drawn ashore, where his jaw was smashed and left gaping.]
> (31/215)
> —Hawaiian saying

V.30 **Kaʻuiki Head**

Volcanic cinder hill

Kaʻuiki ("the glimmering") Head, a 400-foot-elevation cinder hill, was thought to look like a moi (threadfish) and is the place where the legendary ʻAiʻai, son of the fish god Kūʻula, made a koʻa called Makakiloia and a kūʻula (fishstone) for the people. It is believed that this is one of the reasons why the waters around Kaʻuiki attract such a plentiful amount of fish.

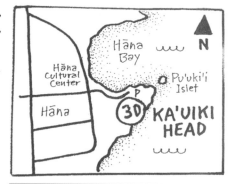

LOCATION: **Makai (ocean side) on Keawa Place, two blocks off Hāna Highway (Route 31), adjacent to the pier at Hāna Bay.**

Hawaiian mythology tells of the great demigod Māui pushing up the sky in return for a drink of water from a young woman here. Clouds may shroud Haleakalā, but they rarely touch Kaʻuiki's summit, thanks to Māui's deed that raised the sky here. Ironically, it has been said that the sky is so low at Kaʻuiki that one can throw a spear into it.

Another legend speaks of how Māui loved the natural beauty of Hāna so much that he named his daughter Noenoe Ua Kea O Hāna ("Misty, Light Rains of Hāna"). Noenoe grew up loving the sea and one day fell in love with Kaʻuiki, the handsome hānai (adopted) son of the menehune. He had been brought to the menehune on the waves and, therefore, these little people believed him to be a blessing from Kanaloa, the god of the sea. Because Ka'uiki was of the sea and kapu, the only way he and Noenoe could be together was for Māui to use his great magic and turn Ka'uiki into a thing of the land. In this way Ka'uiki was changed into the large hill that now graces Hāna Bay, and Noenoe became the misty, gentle rains that, to this day, caress her beloved husband. It is said that the sea repeatedly chants the love story of Noenoe and Ka'uiki as it hugs and jostles the rocky shores of Hāna Bay.

Beneath the rocky cliffs of Ka'uiki, washed by the crashing surf, is the long black body of the giant eel, Laumeki. He swam over from Moloka'i, was killed on the hilltop, and then was thrown down into the sea below the cave, Kekumu o Ka'uiki, where he turned to stone. When the hill trembles, it is due to Laumeki. (Note the similar tale told of Laumeki at Ka Iwi O Pele.)

According to traditional history, Ka'uiki has long been the most defendable position in Hāna during battles between rival forces. Because of its steep cliffs on all but one side, it served warring chiefs as a perfect hill fort. Around 1759, Kalani'ōpu'u of the Big Island captured and held Hāna for some 20 years. In about 1779, Kahekili, the paramount chief of West Maui set

A trail at Hāna Bay leads up to the cave where a plaque marks the spot reputed to be Queen Ka'ahumanu's birthplace.

upon his enemy by sending warriors around both sides of Maui. Kalani'ōpu'u retreated to his stronghold on Ka'uiki hilltop, where he placed a large wooden ki'i (image) with a fierce countenance to frighten the Maui warriors and prevent them from making a night attack. However, it wasn't long before the carved figure was toppled by the Maui forces and the hilltop was conquered. To this day the area mauka of Ka'uiki, where this battle occurred, is called Kāwalaki'i ("fallen image"). Kahekili finally routed Kalani'ōpu'u by stopping up the springs around Ka'uiki Head and the Big Island army was forced to surrender its fortified hilltop due to lack of water. This same strategy had been used in an earlier battle between Big Island chief 'Umi and Lonoapi'ilani of Maui.

The twelfth-century Lahaina chief Hua'apohukaina is associated with two heiau built at the base of Ka'uiki. Honua'ula Heiau, the larger of the two, was visited by him on a journey to Hilo, and Kuawalu Heiau was built by him on his return in thanks for his successful campaign on Hawai'i Island. An imu for burning the bodies of captive warriors was also at this place and was used by Kahekili in 1782. These features are now destroyed.

It was during such unsettled times of warring between Maui and Hawai'i that Ka'ahumanu was born at Hāna. The daughter of Big Island ali'i, Ke'eaumoku and Namahana, she later became the favorite wife of Kamehameha the Great. In 1830, near the end of her life, she pointed out the cave on Ka'uiki in which she had been hidden as a child during the battles between Kalani'ōpu'u of Hawai'i and Kahekili of Maui during the late 1770s. From the pier at Hāna Bay a trail leads up to the cave where a plaque marks the spot of Ka'ahumanu's birth. The trail was badly eroded by rains in 1992, leaving the birth site difficult to access. Every August the favorite queen of the Hawaiian Kingdom is remembered in a solemn festival by Hāna area residents.

At the mouth of Hāna Harbor is a 1.5-acre islet called Pu'uki'i ("image hill"). It is reached by the same trail that leads to Ka'ahumanu's Birthplace, at the right of the pier, and a now dismantled footbridge. A small lighthouse is on the little island's 72-foot summit. This is where 'Umi, the Big Island chief, is said to have erected a huge wooden image to frighten off attackers from the sea. (Note the similarity to the above-mentioned story concerning the later Hawai'i Island chief, Kalani'ōpu'u, and the place called Kāwalaki'i on the other side of Ka'uiki.)

It is recorded that Captain Cook's ships were met by canoes from Hāna in 1778, and that Kamehameha boarded the HMS Resolution off Ka'uiki for a brief sail with Cook before the latter met his fate on the Big Island. In 1802, Kamehameha landed at Hāna Bay with his peleleu ("extended") war fleet, repaired and rededicated several heiau to his war god, Kūkā'ilimoku (making himself the last Hawaiian chief to use Hāna for such purposes), and went on to conquer all of Maui.

Just north of Hāna Bay on a rocky point is an unusual double-temple site, Kauleilepo and Kaulei'ula Heiau. There are also a number of small fishponds in this area called Ka'inalimu ("seaweed procession"). These sites are not accessible as they are on private property. Mauka of Hāna Highway, where the Hāna Medical Center is now located, were formerly the sacred grounds of Kāni'omoku Heiau and pu'uhonua (place of refuge).

Ka'uiki was also used as a lookout for spotting incoming schools of fish. A kilo i'a (fish spotter) signaled to fishermen below where the akule (scad) entered the harbor. Often the entire village joined in a hukilau (pull [net] ropes) when the fish were running. Directed by the kilo i'a, canoes set nets, which the villagers hauled in from the shallow water with enough fish for the whole community.

On the oceanside of Kaʻuiki Head is the strikingly beautiful red sand beach of Kaihalulu. It is a unique wahi pana of Maui.

On the backside of Kaʻuiki Head is the remarkable red sand beach Kaihalulu. It is a clothes-optional beach but the naked beauty is entirely in the place itself. The beach reveals a unique wahi pana, a stuning spirit of place. From the dead end of Ua Kea Street walk across the Hana Community Center lawn to the narrow, sliding cinder trail that skirts the south side of the Head. There are no amenities at this wild beach and you hike in at your own risk.

Please note that Kaʻuiki Head is composed of very loosely packed volcanic cinder that erodes easily and is subject to landslides. When in good condition, trails on Kaʻuiki can be slippery and dangerous. Check with local residents on accessibility of trails. (4/23-25; 22; 23; 32/92, 199; 37/131-139; 40; 43/38, 41, 99, 105-106;)

> I ʻauheʻe ʻo Kaʻuiki i ka wai ʻole.
> Kaʻuiki was defeated for lack of water.
> [When ʻUmi, ruler of Hawaiʻi, went to Hāna to battle against Lonoapiʻilani of Kaʻuiki, thirst weakened the Maui warriors. Often used later to mean "without water or the needed supplies we cannot win."] (28/125)
> —Hawaiian saying

V.31 **Wai'ānapanapa**

Coastal area with numerous archaeological features

Wai'ānapanapa means "glistening water" or "water flashing rainbow hues," and it is here at the water's edge on a weathered 'a'ā lava field, part of the Hāna flow, that a state park of the same name has been established. Supporting dense vegetation, particularly hala (pandanus), false kamani, guava and papaya, Wai'ānapanapa State Park is a beautiful natural region, which is also home to many ancient sites.

When first surveyed in 1969 to ascertain the extent of its archaeological features, Wai'ānap-

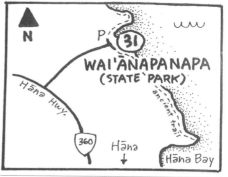

LOCATION: Two miles northwest of Hāna to a sign-posted turn-off, near mile marker 12, then a couple minutes makai to the end of the road, off Hāna Highway. Phone: (808) 984-8106. www.hawaiistateparks.org

anapa revealed 34 ancient sites, including heiau; 5 cave shelters; an ancient trail; one pictograph; 6 ahu; 2 V-shaped shelters; 5 miniature enclosures; 3 shelter walls; 2 house platforms; and numerous burial sites. The 120-acre state park has been developed to include a picnic area, beach facilities with restrooms and showers, a campground, 12 rental-lodging units, a caretaker's residence, and park office.

Two of the six caves at Wai'ānapanapa are featured along a short and enchanting trail cut through a labyrinthine hau grove. Both of these caves appear to be part of the same lava tube, the roof of which collapsed cutting off their connection with each other. The caves contain fresh water that floats on the salt water table and may have been used for washing and preparing food and kapa in former times. These two caves of Wai'ānapanapa also figure in the legend of Pōpō'alaea, wife of the cruel chief Ka'akea. The jealous chief threatened to kill his wife because he disliked the attention she received from her younger brother, Pi'ilani. She fled, with an attendant, to the caves and hid in one of them that could only be entered by swimming under a ledge. One day when Ka'akea was in the area he recognized the distinctive kāhili (feather standard) of his wife's standard reflected in the water at the cave's entrance. Ka'akea brutally murdered Pōpō'alaea and her attendant in a terrible blood bath. Today, the story is told that every spring, on the night of Kū, the fresh water in Wai'ānapanapa Cave turns blood red. At this time of year when the murder occurred, opae ula, red shrimp cover the submerged stones of the cave, turning them brilliant crimson, a reminder of how the gods mark the misdeed that occurred here.

Two of the six caves at Wai'ānapanapa are featured along a short trail cut through a grove of hau trees. The caves contain fresh water that floats on the salt water table and may have been used for washing and preparing food and kapa in former times. The caves are featured in the traditional tale of Chiefess Pōpō'alaea, who was murdered by her jealous husband here.

The high chief Kihaapi'ilani is credited with building the trail that runs through Wai'ānapanapa along the coast and it is therefore named the Kihaapi'ilani Trail. Following the foot path of 'a'ā lava rocks three-quarters of a mile north of the caves will lead one past scattered burial mounds to the temple foundation known as Kaukeali'i Heiau. This large, open platform construction stands about 4 feet high and is 90 feet by 110 feet. Several possible ki'i (image) holes edge the heiau and two ceremonial refuse pits are inside the temple platform. Nothing is known concerning the origin or use of this heiau. A modern

ko'a on the makai side of the clinker trail indicates where the burial sites begin. (Please don't venture off the trail in this area.)

An interesting feature in the park is a painted human figure on a basalt rock face, about .2 miles south of the park cabins. Approximately 65 feet from the ocean and 30 feet mauka of the trail the red pictograph is about five inches tall. The faded image, painted with natural red ochre pigment or possibly kukui nut dye, is 5 feet above ground level. Hawaiian pictographs seem to be an artform almost exclusive to Maui, Moloka'i and Lana'i. It has been suggested that the human figure with flame-like headdress holds a war club in each hand. However, it is more likely that the figure wears some sort of bracelets or ornamental material around its wrists as the three-fingered hands are clearly not grasping anything. The feet are not articulated and the figure appears to be in movement, as if dancing.

A painted human figure appears on a basalt rock face, about five inches tall and painted with natural red ochre pigment (possibly kukui nut dye). It appears that the figure wears some sort of bracelets or ornamental material around its wrists as the three-fingered hands are clearly not grasping anything. The figure also appears to be in movement as if dancing.

About .7 miles south of the park office along the same trail is a small Hale o Lono type heiau called Ohala Heiau, a possible ko'a (fishing shrine). Sixty feet from the ocean's edge at Pa'ina Point and 20 feet from Kihaapi'ilani Trail, this stepped-platform construction is built on a small knoll and reaches a maximum height of some 4 feet. Numerous oblong water-worn stones have been placed in an upright position on and around the heiau, and ti leaf offerings are often in evidence. The east end of the heiau has several hala trees growing on it and a short distance away is the park boundary.

A hike along the stepping-stone, Kihaapi'ilani Trail southward beyond

At the south end of the park is a small Hale o Lono type heiau called Ohala Heiau. It can be found at the south end of the park beside the Kihaapi'ilani Trail at Pa'ina Point.

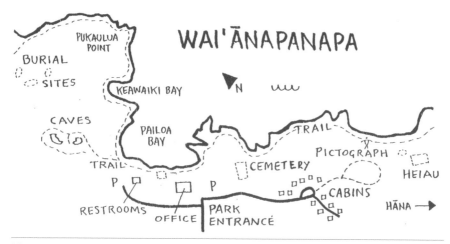

Many other archaeological features can be seen at Wai'ānapanapa. Ask for a map from the park headquarters.

the park will lead into Hāna. Allow two hours for this two-mile coastal hike into Hāna town and look for the trail sections with rhythmically placed, waterworn trail stones. (4/21-22; 17/52-56; 21/71; 30; 32/220-221; 37/125-126; 40; 43/98-99)

V.32 **Pi'ilanihale Heiau**

Extensive stone platform with walled enclosures

(Wikimedia Commons)

According to tradition, Pi'ilani was the first chief to unite all the moku or regions of Maui into one kingdom under single leadership sometime around the sixteenth century. His later reign was subsequently a time of peace and great public works. He is known for the largest heiau in the Hawaiian Islands and the extensive stone-paved footpath that circles the island of Maui. The present Pi'ilani Highway goes over parts of the older trail. Pi'ilani's son Kihaapi'ilani continued this roadwork out along the Hāna coast and even up Kaupō Gap and into Haleakalā Crater (site IV.23).

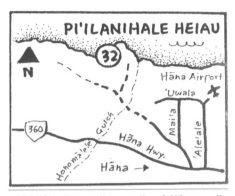

PI'ILANIHALE HEIAU

LOCATION: **Four miles north of Hāna, mile marker 31, along the Hāna Highway. Turn makai on 'Ula'ino Road and drive 1.5 miles; on the right, just past the stream crossing (check water level before crossing). www.ntbg.org**

On Pi'ilani's deathbed he indicated that his oldest son, Lonoapi'ilani, would take over rulership of the Maui kingdom. It was traditional for the oldest son to carry on the hereditary rule and Kihaapi'ilani, the younger son, was raised on O'ahu and had no problem with this until several years into Lonoapi'ilani's reign when the older brother began to resent his younger sibling and finally insulted him. This resentment was apparently related to a visit both brothers had made to the kahuna nui, at the latters invitation. The high priest explained that he was going to reveal to them their goddess and whichever one of them stayed for the entire ritual ceremony, this one would be the true high chief of Maui. The kahuna began to pray and the brothers witnessed a spider spinning a web and seven rainbows appeared in the hale rafters. The spider then dropped down into the imu, earth oven, in the center of the floor as the priest continued to chant. Then the earthen mound of the imu began to rise and Lonoapi'ilani was overwhelmed with fear and dread. As the brothers looked into the fiery imu pit they saw the frightful mo'o goddess Kihawahine in her coiling lizard form. She turned her head and looked directly into the eyes of Lonoapi'ilani and, terrified, he fled the kahuna's hale. The kahuna asked Kihaapi'ilani to prepare 'awa and poi for the goddess and when Kiha looked up from his task he saw Kihawahine in her human form, the most beautiful woman he had ever laid eyes on. Kihawahine whispered to the kahuna nui that Kihaapi'ilani must flee for his life, but with the help of his sister Pi'ikea, wife of Hawai'i High Chief 'Umi, he would return with an army to take Maui from his brother, the one who could not face the goddess.

Pi'ilanihale means "house of Pi'ilani." This name and the size of the heiau indicate that it was built by a mō'ī, or paramount chief. The large luakini heiau, a place of human sacrifice, could only be built and

Pi'ilanihale means "house of Pi'ilani." This name and the size of the heiau indicate that it was probably built by paramount chief Pi'ilani or by his son Kihaapi'ilani in his father's honor.

dedicated by the authority of such a high chief. It may have been Kihaa-pi'ilani who actually dedicated the heiau to his father Pi'ilani.

Pi'ilanihale is the largest known heiau in the Hawaiian Islands, covering nearly three acres and measuring more than 415 feet in length by 340 feet in width. Situated on a large bluff near Kalāhū ("the over-flowing sun") Point in Honomā'ele ("numb bay"), this ancient ritual site is truly awe-inspiring to behold, with the backdrop of Kalapawili Ridge above and the rocky shore below. Along this coastal area surrounding the heiau is dense growth of guava, kukui, and, especially, hau trees. An ancient canoe landing was located at the small black rock beach below the heiau.

There is no other structure quite like this in Hawai'i, with some unusual construction features. The north wall, which is the largest wall of the heiau, has five steeply terraced steps that reach a height of 50 feet. It is constructed of finely fitted lava rock, with some beach stones included but no mortar. In his 1970 survey of Pi'ilanihale Heiau, archaeologist Ross Cordy wrote: "One feature should be noted in connection with this immense retaining wall. Near the horizontal center of the basal step and jutting 0.4 meter horizontally out from it is a large hexagonal, smooth basalt stone. This stone, the base of which is 1.1 meters above ground level, was definitely placed, but for what purpose is unknown."

An excavation, carried out in 1990, radiocarbon-dated the first construction at the site to the late thirteenth century, well before the time of Pi'ilani. A second building phase in the sixteenth century could have seen a rededication of the temple under that chief. A final renovation occurred in the late eighteenth century. Excavations also showed that the heiau was a residential site. The House of Pi'ilani appears to be the homebase of the Pi'ilani lineage.

A path leads up to the temple platform along the northwest corner of the heiau. From within Pi'ilanihale the three enclosures and five platforms can be observed. Two of the stonewall enclosures are rectangular, and one is oval in shape. There are also 23 pits in the lava and beach-stone paving of the heiau and there are numerous upright stones. At the back of the heiau is a well-constructed wall

The north wall, which is the largest wall at Pi'ilanihale Heiau, has five steeply terraced steps that reach a height of over 50 feet. There is no other ancient rockwall construction like this in all of Polynesia.

8 feet in height. Please stay within the viewing areas at the entrance to the heiau, and do not walk on to any of the stone platforms or walls.

The movement of the sun and stars were often observed by means of alignments of rock structures on the heiau. Those built at zero degrees to north aided in knowing the best time for planting. So naturally it is appropriate that this heiau has been incorporated into a private park called Kahanu Gardens, part of the National Tropical Botanical Gardens. Self-guided tours are $10 per person and kamaina are $5, Monday through Friday, 9 AM to 4 PM, Saturdays 9 AM to 2 PM. Guided tours are $25 per person by arrangement, call for reservations: (808) 248-8912. This well-preserved heiau was declared a National Historic Landmark in 1966, and descendants of the Pi'ilani lineage are the present caretakers of the site. (5; 17/53; 21/72-74; 22; 32/184; 37/123; 40; 44/38, 98)

V.33 **Ke'anae**

Natural features

(Wikimedia Commons)

Legend tells us that long ago Maui was a dry and desolate island. Enter Kāne, the god of freshwater sources, accompanied by Kanaloa, god of the sea. Kāne, with his kauila staff, struck a rock at Ke'anae and water came gushing forth providing the land with abundant irrigation. And Kanaloa surrounded the lava peninsula with the plentiful abundance of the sea. This is the mythological account of how farming and fishing became the

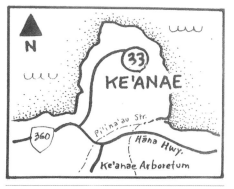

LOCATION: **Off Hāna Highway (route 36), 30 miles west of Kahului, half way to Hāna, near mile marker 17.**

mainstays of Ke'anae. An ancient royal taro patch and fishpond called Ke'anae ("the mullet") near the coastline of the cape is believed to be the origin of the region's name. However, another interpretation refers to the area of Ke'anae as "the Inheritance of Heaven." A legend describes a local chief who wanted to increase his land and food production of taro so he had his people dig and carry tons of earth down the valley to the rough lava tongue that juts into the sea in order to create the now fertile peninsula. The peninsula was actually formed by a swift moving lava flow that descended from Haleakalā's upper crater, through Ko'olau

Gap, and Ke'anae Valley.

After leaving the sugar plantations in the early 1900s, Chinese immigrants began planting rice in the area. Only in the past 25 years, with the revival of Hawaiian cultural identity, have the rice paddies been converted back into the original taro patches. Contemporary Hawaiians now farm taro, bananas, yams and other (wetland) crops here much like their ancestors did before them. However,

Historic Lanakila 'Ihi'ihi O Iēhowa O nā Kaua Church was built in 1860.

little in the way of archaeological excavations have been carried out at Ke'anae, so dating of early settlement has yet to be done.

On the windward side of the half-mile long peninsula is Ke'anae Park and the historic Lanakila 'Ihi'ihi O Iēhowa O nā Kaua Church, built in 1860. The park has no facilities, but is a lovely shoreline location. An ancient canoe landing is still in use today as a small boat ramp, and, although it was restored in 1960, it likely has much the same appearance that it had in earlier times, apart from the concrete additions. Just beyond Pauwalu ("eight destroyed") Point is Mokumana ("divided island") Islet, a seabird sanctuary that rises vertically 40 feet above the choppy coastal waters. Beside it is the smaller Manahoa (needle) Rock. These are the protected homes of many tropical seabirds, including the great frigatebird, white-tailed tropicbird, wedge-tailed shearwater, and the Hawaiian noddy terns. Pauwalu is named for a shark-man that warned groups of fishermen that eight of them were about to die and his prophecies always came true. When Akeake, an early Maui Island hero, heard about this, the shark-man was exposed and destroyed with fire.

At Ke'anae Arboretum, mauka of Hāna Highway, are display gardens and old reconstructed taro patches. Brought to Hawai'i by early Polynesian voyagers, taro has deep cultural and spiritual significance for Native Hawaiians. Of the 200 different varieties, 60 kinds can be found in the arboretum. The corm of the taro plant is cooked and pounded to make a thick paste called poi. Poi served as a main food staple for ancient Hawaiians, along with sweet potatoes, bananas, pork, and fish.

Some of the heiau which have been destroyed or lie in ruin within the Ke'anae area are: Lalaola Heiau, an agricultural temple; Kukui o Lono ("light of Lono") Heiau, a shoreline temple where signal fires were set for seafarers; Pakanaloa Heiau, a platform structure on the upper

Little in the way of archaeological excavations have been carried out at Keʻanae, so dating of early settlements has yet to be done. However, a restored ancient canoe landing can be seen as one enters the peninsula.

slopes of Keʻanae; Kaluanui ("big pit") Heiau, a double section temple of sacrifice from which kapu drums at one time were heard; Kualani Heiau on the west ridge of Waiokāne Falls; and ʻŌhiʻa Heiau, attributed to chief Kaimukī and later broken up and used as a pigpen. These sites are destroyed or inaccessible.

From Wailua Lookout one can see below to the lush Keʻanae Valley, as well as up to the distant Koʻolau Gap slicing through the upland ridge of Haleakalā Crater. (4/19; 17/34-43; 21/70; 32/103; 37/111; 43/91-95)

> ʻO ka wai kau nō ia o Keʻanae; ʻo ka ʻūlei hoʻowali ʻuwala
> ia o Kula.
> It is the pool on the height of Keʻanae; it is the ʻūlei digging
> stick for the potato [patch] of Kula.
> [A handsome young man of Kula and a beautiful young
> woman of Keʻanae, on Maui, were attracted to each other.
> She boasted of her own womanly perfection by referring
> to her body as the pool on the heights of Keʻanae. Not to
> be outdone, he looked down at himself and boasted of his
> manhood as a digging stick of Kula.] (31/267)
> —Hawaiian saying

ANCIENT SITES OF MOLOKA'I

t is said in an ancient Hawaiian chant that after giving birth to the islands of Hawai'i and Maui, Papa, Wākea's first wife, returned to Tahiti. Wākea then took two more wives, Hina, who bore him Moloka'i, and Kaula Wahine who bore Lāna'i. Later, Papa returned to Wākea and gave birth to O'ahu, Kaua'i, Ni'ihau, and finally Kaho'olawe. This is what comes down to us as the traditional explanation of Moloka'i's birth as keiki moku ("island child").

Early spelling of Moloka'i was without the 'okina (glottal stop), thus the meaning of the name Molokai, according to one source, was "the gathering of ocean waters." However, the popular reference to Moloka'i is now as "the Friendly Isle."

The island of Moloka'i lies 8.5 miles northwest of Maui and 9 miles north of Lāna'i. It is the fifth largest of the Hawaiian Islands and stretches 38 miles east to west and 10 miles north to south at its widest point. The island consists of two distincts, each a large volcanic mountain, with a plain connecting them. East Moloka'i is more mountainous with its highest peak, Kamakou, reaching an elevation of 4,970 feet. The northeastern coast is stunningly characterized by high sea cliffs, the tallest in the world, and deep, stream-eroded valleys. This side of the island is considerably wetter than West Moloka'i, which has gulches rather than valleys and has a long, sloping mountain, Maunaloa, that reaches an altitude of 1,380 feet. The western end of the island was an important source of adze stone, a valuable trading commodity in ancient times. There are several adze quarries on Moloka'i's northwestern end. Occasional guided hikes to the Pu'u Kaeo quarry and ancient Hawaiian sites at Mokio Preserve are led by the Moloka'i Land Trust (www.molokailandtrust.org). See also The Nature Conservancy for guided hikes into the coastal sand dunes of Mo'omomi Preserve (www.nature.org), a beautifully wild, natural area.

In earlier times Moloka'i was divided into two political districts: Kona, the dry southern and western region, and Ko'olau, the wetter northeastern area. Between 1859 and 1909, the island was made into one district called Moloka'i. However, the present large land divisions of the island are the districts of Moloka'i (Kona) and Kalawao (Ko'olau), established in 1909.

Moʻomomi Preserve on the northwestern end of Molokaʻi is a beautiful natural area overseen by The Nature Conservancy.

In the tenth century, Molokaʻi became known for its training of powerful kāhuna at Mahana. The select school, known as Kēʻieʻie, was put to the test in the twelfth century, when the Maui warrior chief Kaikololani crossed Pailolo Channel with a great war fleet and attacked Molokaʻi. The people of Molokaʻi were being slaughtered, and, confident of his victory, Kaihololani stopped the battle to hurl verbal abuse at those whom he was about to destroy. Runners were sent to Mahana, and the kāhuna of Kēʻieʻie were begged to give aid to the people of Molokaʻi before it was too late. The old priests hastily traveled to the battle site and, upon seeing so many of their people dead, stood in a circle, in full view of the combatants, and began to pray with their hands raised skyward. Kaikololani and his men continued to threaten and mock the kāhuna, but, when the Maui warriors advanced to fight, they began to fall, one by one, until all but the chief were lying dead on the ground. Kaikololani was allowed to return to Maui with his life, whereupon he told his people of the kāhuna power on Molokaʻi. Ever since then it has been said: "Molokaʻi Pule Oʻo," which means "Molokaʻi of the powerful (ripening) prayers."

Molokaʻi is also known as the birthplace of the hula, a dance form that arose in connection with sacred chants that made Hawaiian oral tradition visible through hand gestures and body movements. The annual Molokaʻi Ka Hula Piko festival is hosted on the island.

The first aliʻi nui (high chief) of Molokaʻi mentioned in traditional chants was Kamauaua, a thirteenth century descendant of the ancient Nanaulu lineage. In the early sixteenth century, Kihaapiʻilani defeated his older brother Lonoapiʻilani for control of Maui with the help of his uncle, ʻUmi, high chief of Hawaiʻi island. ʻUmi advised Kihaapiʻilani how he might become honored by his people and his name live forever: "When you are through on Maui, you will go to Molokaʻi to restore the walls of the fishponds ...This is what will endear you to the people." (35/12) And so the Maui chief is memorialized in part by the great number of fishponds along Molokaʻi's south shore, along the longest fringing reef in the U.S., over 25 miles (see Site 5).

Building and restoring many of the 73 south shore fishponds was one of the great public works that Chief Kihaapi'ilani of Maui carried out for Moloka'i.

Later in the sixteenth century the famous kahuna Lanikaula lived in East Moloka'i, where, in seclusion, he became known for his prophecy and council, reinforcing the reputation of Moloka'i as home to powerful kāhuna. People came to the kukui grove where he lived seeking advice and offering vows, leaving a lock of their hair in a small slit cut in the bark of one of the trees. The hair would stay glued to the trunk by the tree's resin. The original grove covered hundreds of acres, but now, located on private property at Pu'u o Hōkū ("Hill of the Stars"), it is only a few acres in size. Lanikaula was buried in the sacred kukui grove that is known as Ulukukui o Lanikaula (site 2).

By the eighteenth century Moloka'i became involved in the power struggles between Maui, Hawai'i and O'ahu, sometimes being ruled by one or the other. Pakuhiwa Battleground was the site of a 1736 engagement between the armies of Moloka'i, aided by Chief Ala-

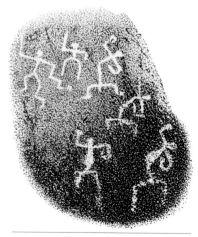

Petroglyphs at Kawela Battleground (site 6) show dancers or possible warriors throwing sling stones. Two famous precontact battles took place in this area.

pa'inui of Hawai'i, and the warriors of Kapi'iohokalani of O'ahu. The site is now called Kawela Battlefield (site 6) because of a later battle in which Kamehameha the Great defeated the fleeing chiefs of Maui in 1792 at nearby Kawela. Once his armies were established on Moloka'i, Kamehameha formed an alliance with the Moloka'i ali'i in hopes of mounting an attack on O'ahu. He also stopped here in order to win Keōpūolani, the granddaughter of defeated Maui chief Kalani'opu'u. She had taken

refuge on the island following her grandfather's death, and Kamehameha wished to have her as his wife as she was a chiefess of the highest rank. Kamehameha was forced to postpone his invasion of O'ahu and return to Hawai'i because of internal trouble at home, and he took Keōpūolani with him. She later bore him two sons, later Kamehameha II and III. Maui high chief Kahekili won back Moloka'i and Lāna'i, and controlled O'ahu with little threat from Kamehameha. Following the death of Kahekili, Kamehameha set out once more to conquer Maui and Moloka'i and finally fulfill his conquest of O'ahu. In 1795 he landed on Moloka'i and faced no opposition. His fleet of war canoes was said to extend along the shore from Kawela to Kamama'ula. Soon after this, all the islands of the archipelago were united as the Hawaiian Kingdom for the first time under Kamehameha.

By the 1860s, King Kamehameha V had established a country estate at Kaunakakai, and Moloka'i

During King Kamehameha V's reign in the 1860s, a leper colony was established on the isolated northshore peninsula of Kalaupapa, seen here from the overlook at Palā'au State Park and looking east from the original settlement site.

was said to be his favorite island. He used his home here, called Mālama (site 7), to escape the "cares of State," and he had a coconut grove planted west of town called Kapuāiwa Coconut Grove (site 8). In 1866, during King Kamehameha V's reign, a leper colony was established on the isolated northshore peninsula of Kalaupapa. The Begium Father Damian, now a saint, helped the desperate Hansen Diseased patients here in the late nineteenth century and the site is presently the Kalaupapa National Historical Park (site 13).

A kūʻula stone and a birthing stone can be seen in front of the Molokaʻi Museum and Cultural Center. Kūʻula stones, named after the fishgod, were considered beneficial to fishermen. Birthing stones were said to relieve labor pains when mothers gave birth on them.

Sandalwood was an important export from Molokaʻi at this time, but was completely depleted by the end of the nineteenth century (site 10). Sugar then came to the island and pineapple in the early twentieth century. The restored R.W. Meyer Sugar Mill recalls this era and is home to the Molokaʻi Museum and Cultural Center. Ranching was an important island industry in the early twentieth century and, along with tourism, remains so today. Less than 4,000 tourists visit Molokaʻi each year.

Molokaʻi has the greatest proportion of Hawaiians of any island, except Niʻihau. About half of its 7,000 people are of Hawaiian lineage. And, although Molokaʻi is known as the "Friendly Isle," this depends on one's own respectful attitude toward the people and the place. (16; 19; 20; 25; 29; 32; 38)

> *Molokaʻi nui a Hina.*
> Great Molokaʻi, land of Hina.
> [The goddess Hina is said to be the mother of Molokaʻi.]
> (31/239)
>
> —Hawaiian saying

Moloka'i Site Map

MOLOKA'I

N

Kauleonānāhoa

13 Kalaupapa

Hālawa Valley

Ho'olehua Airport

12

11

Pāpōhaku

Maunaloa

460

470

Lua Na Moku Iliahi

10

Pōhaku Hāwanawana

1

3

2

Ulukukui Lanikaula

Pōhaku o Kalama'ula

9

Kaunakakai

450

4

8 7

6

5

Kapuāiwa Coconut Grove

Malama

Kawela Battleground

Southshore Fishponds

'Ili'ili'ōpae Heiau

0   10 miles

Moloka'i Site List

1. Hālawa Valley
2. Ulukukui o Lanikaula (Sacred Kukui Grove)
3. Pōhaku o Hāwanawana
4. 'Ili'ili'ōpae Heiau
5. Southshore Fishponds
6. Kawela Battleground
7. Malama (Kamehameha V House Site)
8. Kapuāiwa Coconut Grove
9. Pōhaku o Kalama'ula
10. Lua Na Moku Iliahi (Sandalwood Measuring Pit)
11. Pāpōhaku
12. Kaule o Nānāhoa (Phallic Rock)
13. Kalaupapa

l. Hālawa Valley

Natural setting and archaeological features

One of the most beautiful valleys on Moloka'i, opening out to a small protected bay, Hālawa was home to an extensive ancient settlement dating back possibly to C.E. 600–1100 and is the oldest archaeological site on the island. An archaeological survey and excavation from 1969 to 1970 revealed extensive agricultural features. At one time Hālawa Valley may have supported a population of a thousand people with its intensive agricultural field system, which included some 700 irrigated taro fields.

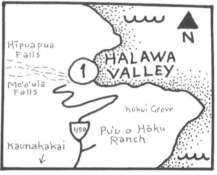

LOCATION: **At the eastern end of Kamehameha V Highway, route 450, 27.5 miles from Kaunakakai.**

The valley floor and slopes are strewn with rock-lined irrigation canals, agricultural terraces, pigpens, house sites and ritual features of various kinds. Two large luakini heiau (temples of human sacrifice), constructed by powerful chiefs, are located in the valley. One, Pāpā Heiau, an arrangement of rock terraces, platforms and enclosures, is said to have been a center for training kāhuna (priests). The other, Mana Heiau, up on the northern slopes of the valley, is a large stone

At one time Hālawa Valley may have supported a population of a thousand people with its intensive agricultural field system, which included some 700 irrigated taro fields.

platform with a 13-foot-high terraced façade. It was built by the Hawai'i Island warrior Chief Alapainui, following a war in which he went to the aid of the Moloka'i Kona district chiefs in their battle against the Ko'olau district armies. No fewer than two-dozen heiau and a pu'uhonua (place of refuge) were built in Hālawa. The small bay at Hālawa served as a good canoe landing, and it was said to be the second favorite spot for Moloka'i chiefs to show off their surfing skills.

When it is particularly wet in Hālawa there are nine waterfalls. The main falls is refered to as Moa'ula. A 1.5-mile trail leads up along the stream and into the valley past numerous rock walls and archaeological sites to Moa'ula Falls (250 ft.) and Hīpuapua Falls (500 ft.). It is said that the pool below Moa'ula Falls is inhabited by a giant mo'o from whom one asks permission before swimming in the cool mountain waters of the pool. In fact, the traditional name of the falls is apparently Mo'o 'Ula ("red lizard") not Moa'ula ("red chicken"). According to local legend, one places a single kī (ti) leaf in the water and if it floats it means permission is granted to swim; but, if it sinks, one swims at one's own risk. However, according to kahu Pilipo Solatorio, who grew up in the valley and survived the 1946 tsunami, the actual practice of consulting the mo'o is to anchor an entire stalk of kī with a small stone and float it in the right side of the pool. If it sinks it means the mo'o (spirit of the

Hālawa Valley has nine waterfalls but two main falls, Moaʻula or Moʻoʻula Falls (250 ft.) on the left and Hīpuapua Falls (500 ft.) on the right. It is said that the pool below Moʻoʻula Falls is inhabited by a giant moʻo from which the falls Moʻo ʻUla ("red lizard") gets its name. (Photo by Nickolai Browne)

water) is present and one should not disturb it.

In 1965, a flashflood altered the course of the river and reduced the amount of farming done in the valley. Only about a dozen permenant residents live in Hālawa at present. The valley is privately owned and there have been disputes over trail access. However, guided tours can be arranged locally. Pilipo Solatorio and his son Greg offer guided hikes of Hālawa several days a week. Phone: (808) 542-1855. www.halawavalleymolokai. com. The beach is public and accessible. (19/70; 21/52; 38/160)

According to kahu Pilipo Solatorio, who grew up in the valley and survived the 1946 tsunami, no one was killed in the tidal wave but it changed Halawa Valley forever.

2. Ulukukui o Lanikaula (Sacred Kukui Grove)

Natural setting

It was in the time of the 16th century Chief Kamalalawalu of Maui that legend tells us how Moloka'i was the island of the most powerful kāhuna, especially those versed in sorcery. It is said that this powerful mana (spiritual power) was due to the goddess Pahulu who overshadowed Maui, Moloka'i and Lāna'i before the time of Pele, when the gods Kāne and Kanaloa first came to the islands.

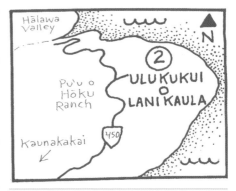

LOCATION: **At the eastern end of Kamehameha V Highway, route 450, 27.5 miles from Kaunakakai.**

Lanikaula, a kahuna and kaula (prophet), made his home at the eastern end of Moloka'i in a kukui grove above Halawa Valley at a place known as Pu'u o Hōkū (Hill of the Stars). It is said that at one time he went over to Lāna'i and killed all of the akua who were related to Pahulu, except for three. These surviving spirits, Kāneikaulanaula (Kāne in the red sunset), Kāneikahuilaokalani (Kāne in the lightning), and Kapo, came to Moloka'i and entered into three trees where suddenly 400 trees sprang up.

Lanikaula ("divine prophet") was very cautious about how he did things so that rival kāhuna could not get the better of him. He was very careful to hide his kūkae (excrement) for this reason and took it out to a small islet just offshore to be secretly buried. Kawelo of Lāna'i came to learn from Lanikaula, spied on him and discovered that the kahuna went each day to the little island of Mokuho'oniki to secret his waste. So Kawelo snatched some of the by-product, hid it in a hollowed-out 'uala (sweet potato), and back on Lāna'i threw it on his sacred fire (see Lāna'i site 4). Seeing a purple-black smoke above Lāna'i, it was then that Lanikaula knew he would die. He called his sons together in order to figure out what method of burial would be best to hide his bones. His sons all came up with unsatisfactory ideas until his youngest son suggested he should be buried in a pit and his bones covered with stones. It is believed he is buried in the kukui grove named for him, Ulukukui o Lanikaula ("Kukui Grove of Lanikaula"). According to the legend, Kawelo of Lāna'i later threw himself off the cliffs at Maunalei and killed himself.

Kukui (Aleurites moluccanus) or candlenut is the Hawai'i state tree and is the representative plant of Moloka'i Island. Kukui is a symbol of enlightenment, protection and peace. The nuts were burned to provide light, thus the name candlenut. They burn for about 15 minutes and were often used in this way to mark time. The shells, leaves and flowers were strung to make leis; the oil and charred nuts were used as pigment, dye and ink for pictograms, kapa and tattoos, respectively. Fishermen would chew the nuts and spit them on the water to reduce surface reflection and increase underwater visibility. They would also use the oil on their nets in order to preserve them against water damage. Canoe seats and gunwales were often made from kukui wood. The demigod Kamapua'a, who could turn himself into a pig, a flower, or a fish, could also take the form of a kukui tree.

Ulukukui o Lanikaula is located on the private lands

Kukui (Aleurites moluccanus) or candlenut is the Hawai'i state tree and is the mascot plant of Moloka'i Island. Kukui is a symbol of enlightenment, protection and peace. It is believed the kahuna Lanikaula is buried in the kukui grove named for him, Ulukukui o Lanikaula ("Kukui Grove of Sky Prophet").

of Pu'u o Hōkū Ranch and can only be visited with permission. However, 2,887 acres of the 13,000-acre ranch, including the grove and 3-miles of coastal lands, were signed over as a conservation easement with the Hawaiian Island Land Trust in 2006. The original royal land grant to Paul Fagan has stayed in tact under the present owner and with the recent easement promises to protect and conserve the cultural sites and natural resources in this area while continuing to operate as a certified organic and biodynamic cattle ranch. Visits to the grove are restricted. Advanced arrangements are required. (12; 14; 21; 29; 32; 38)

3. Pōhaku Hāwanawana

Boulder

The story goes that the "Whispering Stone," Pōhaku Hāwanawana, was a place where fishermen would stop on their way to the coast below and softly make requests for help in catching fish. If the fishermen wanted taro, they whispered this to the stone and upland farmers would bring taro to trade for fish. When farmers wanted fish, they, too, would whisper to the stone and their wishes would likewise be heard. The stone is also said to be a boundary marker.

The rectangular stone stands, almost 6 feet tall and 3 feet wide, near Pōhakupili Gulch on the eastern side of the road. The pole for a Hawai'i Visitors Bureau sign is in front of the stone, but no sign remains. Some local Hawaiians say this is not the real Pōhaku Hāwanawana, that the authentic whispering stone is further down the gulch toward the ocean. However, it is also said that there are a number of whispering stones running from the coast and up the hillside. In this way, the stones could whisper their messages more easily, one to the other. This particular stone is the most accessible whispering stone. Do not stop in the roadway if you wish to see Pōhaku Hāwanawana, pull over on to the grass. (29; 38)

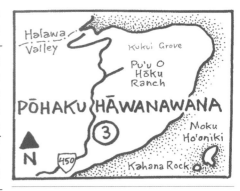

LOCATION: **Twenty-five yards south of the 23-mile marker along the makai side of Kamehameha V Highway, Route 450. It is difficult to spot when driving uphill, but on your return, watch for the 23-mile marker and look just beyond and at the top of the embankment. There are no shoulders for parking, but there is some room on the grass. Do not stop on the highway.**

4. 'Ili'ili'ōpae Heiau

Rock temple platform

'Ili'ili'ōpae (also 'Ili'ili'ōpoe and 'Ili'ili'ōpoi) is the largest and oldest heiau on Moloka'i. It is considered by some Hawaiians to be the piko (navel) of Moloka'i and of all the Hawaiian Islands. Said to be built by menehune at the time of Chief Ka'alauohua, from north shore stones carried over the mountains from Wailau Valley, it was constructed in one night. The menehune received payment in food; one shrimp ('ōpae) per worker.

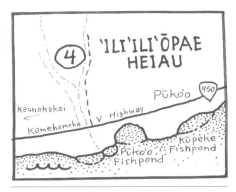

LOCATION: **Not far from mile marker 16 on Kamehameha V Highway (450), out of Kaunakakai, just past Mapulehu Bridge and up a gated dirt road, half a mile, on the left.**

It is also said that in the fourteenth century Umoekekaua lived in this area with his 10 sons. Over time, nine of the sons were sacrificed at the heiau by the priests 'Ōpiopio and 'Ai'ai. Following the loss of his ninth son, Umoekekaua and his last son sought the aid of Kauhuhū, the shark god, who, in response, sent a flood down the valley inundating the land. The flash flood destroyed the temple (which was much larger in size in those days, measuring 920 feet long) and swept Chief Ka'alauohua, 'Ōpiopio, 'Ai'ai, and all the other kāhuna out to sea, where they were devoured by sharks.

In another, similar story the kahuna Kamalō called on the shark god to avenge the deaths of his two sons who were sacrificed at the heiau for playing the sacred drums. A storm came and washed all the people out to sea, except for Kamalō and his family.

Chief 'Aikānaka is said to have rebuilt the heiau using many of the original stones. The heiau presently measures 287 feet long by 87 feet wide. Its rock platform stands between 11 and 22 feet above the ground, with three well-built terraces on the eastern end. There is one terrace on

'Ili'ili'ōpae Heiau, the largest heiau on Moloka'i, stands 22-feet high in places, with three well-built terraces on the eastern end. There is one terrace on the western end of the temple.

'Ili'ili'ōpae is the largest and possibly the oldest heiau on Moloka'i. It is considered by Hawaiians to be the piko (navel) of Moloka'i and of all the Hawaiian Islands. Few original features exist on the platform, but it is said that wooden ki'i (images) representing the gods Kūkā'ilimoku and Lono were erected on the central platform.

the western end of the temple. Few original features exist on the platform, but it is said that wooden ki'i (images) representing the gods Kūkā'ilimoku (Kū) and Lono were erected on the central platform, with images of the gods Kalia and Uli fixed at the second and first terrace levels. The heiau is part of a larger National Historic Landmark that includes six heiau and two fishponds and is known as Hokukano-Ualapue Complex. It was added to the National Register of Historic Places in 1966. A trail leading from the heiau use to run up and over the ridge all the way over to Wailau Valley on the other side of the mountain but is now completely overgrown and inaccessible.

When the heiau was larger in size, it was said to be a training college for powerful kāhuna. Later, after renovations, it was used for sacrifices during the season of Kāne, between the twenty-fourth and twenty-seventh days of the moon. Only human males, pigs, dogs, fowl, and bananas were offered. The people were summoned by drums and all male members of the family gathered at the base of the temple while women stayed away. Mats were placed on the stone foundation of the temple during ceremonies. When the offering was carried to the temple, all fell down to the ground as the sacrifice was killed by stran-

The last person to worship at 'Ili'ili'ōpae Heiau was persuaded by Father Damien to come to his church, St. Joseph's. She was converted to Christianity and the ancient temple fell into disuse.

gulation. The ceremony took about a day to perform and the victim's body was burned a short distance from the temple.

According to local tradition, the last person to worship openly at the heiau, an old woman named Kī'ili'ohe, was persuaded by Father Damien to come to his church, St. Joseph's. Kī'ili'ohe was so moved by the service that she converted to Christianity. 'Ili'ili'ōpae was abandoned and gradually fell into disrepair.

'Ili'ili'ōpae Heiau lies at the base of a ridge, tucked between the two forks of Mapulehu Stream not far from Pūko'o. A Hawai'i Visitor's Bureau sign use to stand beside the highway but has long since disappeared. Because the heiau is on private land, access is restricted, but signage for the site can be found at the first gated dirt road past Mapelahu Stream. Please respect this and all ancient sites. (19/60; 20/131-132; 38/130-34)

5. **South Shore Fishponds**

Pond walls

Throughout all of Oceania, only the ancient Hawaiians developed a true aquaculture that went beyond mere trapping and evolved into an elaborate and extensive industry of fish husbandry. Sluice gates known as mākāhā were constructed to let fingerlings into enclosed bays and springfed ponds retaining bigger, mature fish as a ready food supply for ali'i and commoners.

Kihaapi'ilani, high chief of Maui, was advised by his brother-in-law, 'Umi, high chief of Hawai'i Island, that, once he had put things in order on Maui, he should go to Moloka'i and restore the walls of the fishponds to become famous and preserve his memory in the minds of the people. This, Kihaapi'ilani did, together with building a road lined with white seashells (to help night travelers) on Moloka'i and Maui, and these deeds endeared him to his people. Building and repairing the fishponds

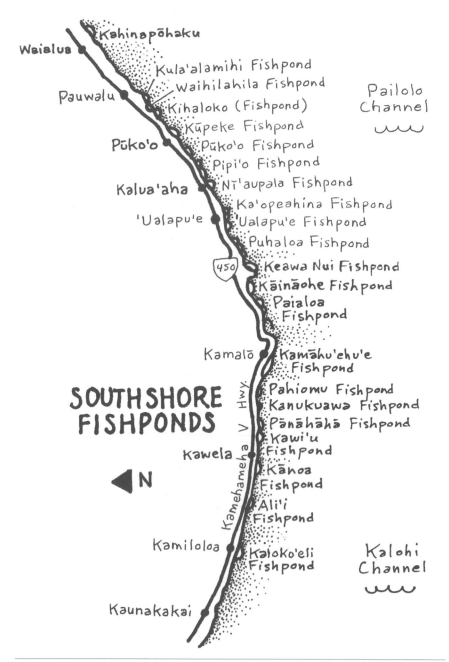

Kahinapōhaku

Waialua

Kula'alamihi Fishpond

Waihilahila Fishpond

Pailolo Channel

Pauwalu

Kihaloko (Fishpond)

Kūpeke Fishpond

Pūko'o

Pūko'o Fishpond

Pipi'o Fishpond

Kalua'aha

Nī'aupala Fishpond

Ka'opeahina Fishpond

'Ualapu'e

Ualapu'e Fishpond

Puhaloa Fishpond

450

Keawa Nui Fishpond

Kāināohe Fishpond

Paialoa Fishpond

Kamalō

Kamāhu'ehu'e Fishpond

Pahiomu Fishpond

Kanukuawa Fishpond

Pānāhāhā Fishpond

Kawi'u Fishpond

Kawela

Kānoa Fishpond

Ali'i Fishpond

Kamiloloa

Kaloko'eli Fishpond

Kalohi Channel

Kaunakakai

Kamehameha V Hwy.

SOUTH SHORE FISHPONDS

◄ N

LOCATION: **Coastal side of Kamehameha V Highway (450) between Kaunakakai and Honouli Wai, just beyond Waialua. Be aware that most of the ponds should not be walked upon or trespassed but viewed from a respectable distance.**

In ancient times, along a 25-mile stretch of Molokaʻi's leeward coastline, there were between 60 and 73 fishponds. Many of them can still be seen today. The island of Maui is visible on the horizon beyond this productive fishpond; pond walls need regular maintenance and youth groups and community groups often help with this work; smaller holding ponds for fingerlings were sometimes built beside the larger fishponds.

of Moloka'i was no small task, for along the Kona (leeward) coast there were dozens of "houses where the fish live," hale o ka i'a e noho ai.

These south shore fishponds were so valuable that the people of the Ko'olau (windward) district, where ocean fishing was too dangerous for half the year because of rough seas, often attacked their south shore neighbors in hopes of gaining possession of the fishponds. The Ko'olau armies were eventually defeated in the early eighteenth century, when the O'ahu chief, Kuali'i, joined forces with the Kona chiefs and united the entire island of Moloka'i.

There are five different types of fishponds: loko i'a kalo, loko wai, loko pu'uone, loko kuapā, and loko 'ume iki. See the section on Types of Sites: Fishponds at the beginning of this book for more information.

Although the island of O'ahu had more fishponds than any of the other Hawaiian Islands, Moloka'i, along this 25-mile stretch of its sheltered leeward coast, had as many as 70 ponds. Many of these

Along a 25-mile stretch of Moloka'i's sheltered leeward coast as many as 73 ponds once thrived. Many of these fishponds can still be seen today as one drives along Kamehameha V Highway.

fishponds can still be seen today as one drives along Kamehameha V Highway, east of Kaunakakai. Many of these ponds are private property so please view ponds from afar and do not trespass or walk on pond walls. (19/45-47; 21/51; 38/12; 41)

> *Moloka'i ko'o lā'au.*
> Moloka'i of the canoe-poler.
> [The reef at the southern shore of Moloka'i extends out as far as one-half mile in some places. At low tide the water is no more than eight feet deep. Because it is so shallow, the people could propel their canoes with poles.] (31/238)
> —Hawaiian saying

6. Kawela Battleground

Natural setting

Kawela means "the heat" and is the name of the ahupua'a (land division) where a great pre-contact battle took place around 1736 between the joint forces of the Moloka'i and Hawai'i Island and the superior invading army of O'ahu. After five days of fierce hand-to-hand warfare the O'ahu chief Kapi'ioho'okai was killed and his army routed. The number of human bones found by archaeologists in this area indicate that thousands were killed in the fighting. Locals state that the wandering spirits of the Night Marchers still haunt this

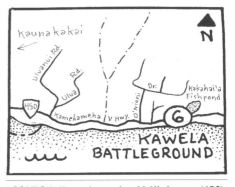

LOCATION: **Kamehameha V Highway (450), 5 miles east of Kaunakakai, between mile marker 5 and 6. A Visitor's Bureau sign sometimes marks the general battleground area but it marches off from time to time.**

area to this day. The site is also known as Pakuhiwa Battleground for still earlier fighting that took place in the area.

In 1794, the Hawai'i Island forces of Kamehameha the Great landed here after conquering Maui. In his sweep to unite all of the islands a fleet of war canoes lined the coast for miles and Kamehameha's army met with little resistence. He took the young Keōpūolani ("gathering of the clouds of heaven"), a very highborn princess, granddaughter of Ha-

Petroglyphs in the Kawela Battleground area depict human figures flexing their muscles, fishhooks, dogs (one dog being led on a leash by a human figure), and rows of possible marching warriors or fleeing people. (Photos by Kay Hirayama)

wai'i Island chief Kalani'opu'u, as his wife. Their sons would later rule the unified Kingdom of Hawai'i.

In the 19th century, this area would be a part of the extensive Moloka'i Ranch, owned by King Kamehameha V. Today, subdivisions and vacation homes occupy the battleground and the remnants of an ancient fishpond can be seen. The fishpond and wetlands are preserved as part of the Kakahai'a National Wildlife Refuge and Maui County maintains the adjacent Kakahai'a Park.

There are over 20 archaeological features in the area that are listed on the National Register of Historic Places. They include ancient house sites, argricultural fields and irrigation ditches, burials, petroglyph rock carvings, religious structures, walls, the fishpond, a fortified complex and a pu'uhonua (place of refuge). These sites are in a conservation area and are not easily accessible to the public but the former battle area can be well imagined from the coastline up into the surrounding gulches and hills. There is no historical marker to indicate the battleground. (15; 20; 22; 29; 38)

7. Malama (Kamehameha V House Site)

House foundation

This neglected historic site was where King Kamehameha V (1830-1872) had his summer "palace" and where he temporarily escaped the worries of the Hawaiian Kingdom and the affairs of state. It was a modest grass hale (house) that he called Malama ("Light"). A highly polished post stood out in front of the hale with hooks for hanging fish, poi, and other food supplies. The smooth surface of the pole prevented rats from getting at the parishables. The post was still in situ just before the Second World War.

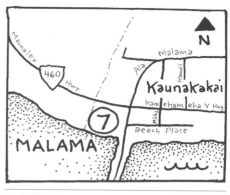

LOCATION: **South, out of town on Kaunakakai Road, toward the pier. The house site is on the grounds of the Moloka'i Canoe Club (private) and can be seen from the road.**

The king built his house on the foundation of an old heiau site and ordered its entrance to face the rising sun, its exit toward the setting

The king built his house on the foundation of an old heiau site and ordered its entrance to face the rising sun, its exit toward the setting sun, which was kapu according to tradition. The people later admired the king for the intelligent way in which he bypassed the old kapu.

sun, which was kapu according to tradition. The workmen protested but the king insisted on having it his way. When it came time for the house blessing and all the people were gathered it was clear that the kapu had been broken. The kāhuna and ali'i scolded their monarch for his transgression and said it would surely mean his death. But King Kamehameha V pointed out that although the hale doorways faced east and west the actual entrance steps up the foundation faced the ocean (south) and therefore did not break the ancient tradition. The people then greatly admired the king for the intelligent way in which he out-smarted the old kapu.

Mark Twain, who visited Hawai'i in 1866, said of King Kamehameha V: "He was a wise sovereign; he had seen something of the world; he was educated and accomplished, and he tried hard to do well by his people, and succeeded. There was no trivial royal nonsense about him; He dressed plainly, poked about Honolulu, night or day, on his old horse, unattended; he was popular, greatly respected, and even beloved."

Before he was king, Kapuāiwa (his given name) held various ministerial positions in his brother King Kamehameha IV's government. He often entertained friends and royalty such as John Dominis (husband of later Queen Lili'uokalani), Chief Ke'eaumoku, and other ali'i nui. They often enjoyed sunbathing at Royal Sands, the beach fronting the Malama house site, as it wasn't a swimming beach. One of the visiting foreign dignitaries who was on Moloka'i to advise the kingdom how to replace the now exhausted sandalwood trade suddenly came up with the idea of salt production while sunbathing with Kapuāiwa. Under his direction salt pans were constructed beside the ocean's edge, letting salt water into the pans, which then evaporated in the sun and left a thin layer of white salt until, after numerous tidal flows into the pans, there was enough salt to scoop out, bag and sell. This proved to be a good business venture for the kingdom. Because it was the flowing ocean water that allowed this venture to succeed, the visiting dignitary suggested the place be called kaunakahakai ("current of the sea"). Today, this area is called Kaunakakai ("town by the sea"). (4; 29; 38)

8. **Kapuāiwa Coconut Grove**

Natural setting

It is said that King Kamehameha V, owner of the vast Moloka'i Ranch, planted 1000 coconut trees in 1863 on a 10-acre coastal stretch of land near the village of Kaunakakai. Each tree was to represent a warrior in the royal armed forces. Kapuāiwa was the king's given name before he was crowned monarch of the Kingdom of Hawai'i and took the family name of Kamehameha. However, there are records showing that Rudolph W. Meyer, the Moloka'i Ranch manager, organized the planting of Kapuāiwa Coconut Grove in 1854.

This is a sacred place in part because of the plentiful flow of subterranean springs directly beneigth the grove. These freshwater springs make the ground unstable and can be seen gushing out in rivulets and pools and then into the ocean. Wai (water) was considered valuable. Thus waiwai means "wealth" in Hawaiian. There are five springs here; the farmers' spring, for those who worked the land to bathe in after a hard days work; the community spring, the largest one, where the farmers would go after washing to join the fishermen and the women and children; the drinking-water spring, with its fresh, "sweet water"; the fourth spring was for cleaning the catch from the sea; and the fifth sping was for menstruating women who were forbidden in the community spring. Each month the water of the fifth spring would turn red.

Today there are only a few hundred trees left in the grove due to neglect and disease. Over the years the grove has been replanted at least three times. The Department of Hawaiian Home Lands has fenced off the grove for safety reasons but it can still be accessed by adjacent Kiowea Beach Park or viewed from the highway. (29; 38)

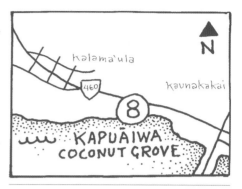

LOCATION: **Coastal side of Kamehameha IV Highway (450), half a mile west of Kaunakakai, across from Church Row.**

Kapuāiwa Coconut Grove is a sacred place in part because of the plentiful subterranean springs that run below the grove. These freshwater springs can be seen gushing out in rivulets and pools, disappear again underground, and flow into the ocean.

Today there are only a few hundred trees left in Kapuāiwa Coconut Grove due to neglect and disease. Over the years parts of the grove have been replanted at least three times.

9. Pōhaku o Kalamaʻula

Boulder

According to legend, the daughter of a Moloka'i chief was in love with a commoner. This was kapu (forbidden). The couple met regularly together by a large boulder in the area outside of present day Kaunakakai called Kalama'ula. When the chief found out about the platonic relationship he forbid them from meeting again. They both knew their love was doomed but they wanted to meet once more beside their rock. The chief refused them this one last meeting but the daughter went anyway to wait for her loved one. However, the young man could not disobey

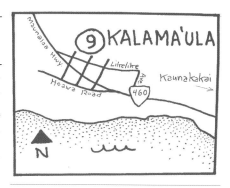

LOCATION: **From Kamehameha IV Highway (450), three quarters of a mile west of Kaunakakai, turn right on Kalanianaole Avenue and proceed to the end of the road.**

his chief and so he didn't make the appointed rendezvous. The young ali'i maiden fell asleep at the boulder while awaiting her lover but was not awakened by him. When she awoke in the morning she struck the stone and exclaimed that the rock would be called Kalama'ula because she was awakened not by her beloved but by the red rays of the rising sun. She further declared that the stone must stay there forever and in that moment the sun burned five red rays into the rock which can still be seen today.

When the princess awoke in the morning she called the stone Kalama'ula because she was awakened by the red rays of the rising sun. She declared that the stone would not be moved from this spot and in that moment the sun burned five red rays into the rock which can still be seen today.

Centuries later, this area became the first Hawaiian Home Lands settlement in the islands when in 1921 a law was passed to give former Royal Crown lands to Native Hawaiians as homesteads. A family that was awarded land at Kalama'ula tried to dig up the boulder for it was blocking their driveway. But it would not budge. Later, when the neighborhood was to be extended a road crew was going to blast the boulder out with dynamite but when they were told the story of Pōhaku o Kalama'ula they left the ancient rock in the middle of the road where it remains to this day. The roadway splits to go around the stone and a metal guard rail protects the boulder. Pōhaku o Kalama'ula means "Stone of the Red Light." (29)

10. Lua Na Moku Iliahi (Sandalwood Measuring Pit)

Historic trench

This historic, not ancient site, Lua Na Moku Iliahi is a 75-foot-long, boat-shaped trench dug in the early 1800s by order of the Hawaiian Kingdom when the sandalwood trade was at its peak. Sandalwood was first discovered in Hawai'i in the 1790s and within the next few decades the Hawaiian king's paid for imported foreign goods with this sweet smelling timber which was highly valued as a trade item in China. Kamehameha the Great, who had united the Hawaiian Islands, controlled the sale of the trees but following his death there was a wholesale pillaging of the highly prized wood. Shiploads of the scented wood were cleared from the upland forests of all the islands until after a few decades there was nothing left. While he was alive, Kamehameha wisely placed a kapu on the young trees and made no transactions on credit. Trade for western goods, particularly weapons and ammunition, are what eventually gave Kamehameha his advantage over other island adversaries. It is recorded that in 1817 he traded two shiploads of sandalwood for the fighting brig Columbia.

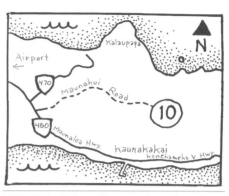

The cut timber would be measured by rolling the logs into a pit the size of a 19th century ship's hold. Men would then haul the logs downhill to the awaiting

LOCATION: **3.5 miles northwest out of Kaunakakai on Highway 460, turn right on Maunahui Road and proceed 9.8 miles on an unpaved road. 4WD is required to visit this site.**

ships. But the sons of Kamehameha were not as good at trading as their shrewd father and they soon went into debt with the sandalwood merchants. As supplies of sandalwood began to dwindle and the precious cargo became harder to find entire forests would be set fire in order to locate the special wood by its perfumed aroma. This didn't damage the large trees but it wiped out the seedlings. Not a very ecological practice. By the 1830s the sandalwood trade was finished.

There are still some sandalwood trees in isolated places on the island but the sandalwood trade was exhausted by the 1830s.

One mile beyond the Lua (pit) is the Waikolu Lookout and Picnic Area. There are picnic tables, toilets, no water, and an amazing panoramic view of the canyon below, sea cliffs, and offshore islands. There is hunting of wild pigs, goats, and axis deer (the latter a gift from India) on weekends and holidays so stay on the trail, wear bright colored clothing, and don't make animal noises. (19; 38)

11. **Pāpōhaku**

Natural setting

There is an ancient tale that tells of an east Moloka'i chief who set off in his canoe with some of his people around the island. As they paddled past west Moloka'i they came upon some fishermen of that area who had a large catch of 'ōpelu (mackerel scad). Because the paddlers were hungry they immediately set upon eating the fish. The fishermen were agast and informed the hungry strangers that these fish were kapu (forbidden) to chiefs in this part of the island. The visiting chief immediately fell ill. The fishermen took him and his crew

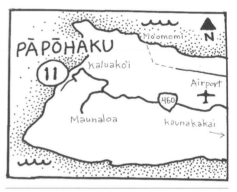

LOCATION: **Pāpōhaku Beach Park is 12 miles from Kaunakakai, and 5 miles down Kalu-ako'i Road from the junction of Maunaloa Highway (480).**

to their local kahuna who said that only if some one else was sacrificed could the chief live. One of the chief's men volunteered to give his life and so the chief eventually recover. The victim was buried on the beach and a tree was planted at the spot. But the grateful chief wanted to better commemorate the man who gave his life that he might live, so he had his men build a fifty-foot long stonewall. But this still was not enough.

He had his men build it two hundred feet longer and the chief put the last stone into the wall. During the winter months the surf carries much of the sand beach away and exposes a natural rock ledge below the sand and the ancient geological "wall" can be seen. This is how the beach got its name, Pāpōhaku, "stone wall."

Archaeological finds in Pāpōhaku indicate a populated settlement with house sites, fish shrines, and a heiau was on Pu'u o Kaiaka, the promontory overlooking Pāpōhaku Beach. Three hōlua (sled ramps) were just inland.

Based on the archaeological finds in the area, Pāpōhaku was a more populated settlement area in ancient times than the nearby Kaluako'i. There are destroyed house sites, fish shrines, and a heiau was on Pu'u o Kaiaka, the promontory overlooking Pāpōhaku Beach. Three hōlua (sled ramps) were just inland from here at Pu'u Kulua. Today, besides the natural beauty of the beach, the only visible archaeological features one might find is the pavement of abandoned golf cart paths from the 1970s when a golf course and safari park were in this area.

A grateful chief commemorated the man who gave his life that the chief might live by building a two hundred foot-long stonewall on Pāpōhaku ("stone wall") Beach. During the winter months the surf exposes a natural rock ledge below the sand, an ancient geological "stone wall."

Pāpōhaku is the site of the annual Moloka'i Ka Hula Piko, a hula festival established by the late Kumu Hula John Ka'imikaua. It honors Hawaiian traditions and practices while celebrating the origin and birthplace of hula. (38)

12. **Kaule o Nānāhoa (Phallic Rock)**

Boulders, petroglyphs, hōlua

The finest example of a phallic rock in the Hawaiian Islands, Kaule o Nānāhoa, "the penis of Nānāhoa," is prominently featured on the summit of Nānāhoa Hill, also known as Pu'u Lua, at an elevation of 1,560 feet. Before reforestation of the area in the 1930s, Kauleonānāhoa could be seen for miles around, proud and erect, pointing to the heavens.

According to legend, during a difficult time when the population had dwindled due to fighting, the chiefs consulted their kāhuna

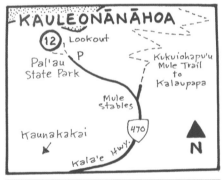

LOCATION: **At the end of Kala'e Hwy. (470), in Pālā'au State Park. From the parking lot, follow the trail to the left about 150 yards.**

and were advised by the gods to send all the women who were not with child to make offerings at Kauleonānāhoa and spend the night by the stone. This was done, and all the women returned home pregnant. So effective is the stone's mana that it is said that some Moloka'i women to this day don't go near the site for fear of getting pregnant.

Another story tells of an ali'i named Nānāhoa who lived on the hill. His wife caught him with another woman and in her rage she pushed the mistress off the nearby pali. Nānāhoa and his wife were turned to stone, and they can both be seen frozen in time on the hill as a lesson to all.

Throughout the ancient world, phallic stones were believed to possess procreative male energy, which could be passed on in the form of fertility. The Hindu lingam stones of India, dedi-

A companion boulder in the form of a large female genital, called Kawahuna, lies not far from her male counterpart. It is said that as long as Kawahuna is there so Kaule o Nānāhoa will stand erect.

cated to Shiva, are examples of this. Celtic peoples set large stones upright to mark the places of power where they could contact their ancestors. Throughout Hawai'i, stones were likewise set upright at heiau and were often associated with the creator god, Kāne. Such stones are referred to as pōhaku o Kāne.

The Kaule o Nānāhoa stone is about 15 feet long and about 5 feet from the tip of its head to the ground at its base, although it appears much taller because of the sloping ground. It is a natural rock formation with the possibility of some artificial shaping having been carried out. A companion boulder in the form of a large female genital, called Kawahuna, lies to the southwest of her male counterpart. It is said that, as long as Kawahuna, also known as Nāwa'akaluli and Waihu'ehu'e, is there, so Kauleonānāhoa will stand erect.

Numerous small, engraved stones fashioned to resemble female genitalia have been found at this site of Kaule o Nānāhoa. These artifacts, which are now in the Bishop Museum in Honolulu, are thought to have been placed at the phallic rock to receive mana from it. Later, they would be taken home to help promote better crop productivity and animal fertility.

Also nearby are several large wind-eroded boulders with more than

More than two-dozen petroglyphs are etched into a large boulders along the path to Kaule o Nānāhoa. Lightly abraded, mostly human figures, range in size from 5 to 24 inches. Most of these figures are no longer discernable due to weathering and vandalism. One must look very closely at the right time of day when the sun is at an angle.

In ancient times Nānāhoa Hill was not overgrown like it is today. When the hilltop was bare there was an hōlua course, a slide, visible which extended from the Phallic Rock over 200 feet down the southern slope as can be seen in this photograph from 1919. Unlike many other hōlua sled courses, this one was not paved. A long wooden sled was ridden down the incline by ali'i in contests of courage and skill. (Photo by J. Stokes, Bishop Museum)

two-dozen petroglyphs on them. Lightly abraded, the mostly human figures range in size from 5 to 24 inches. Most of these figures are no longer discernable due to weathering and vandalism. Also on Nānāhoa Hill is a now-overgrown hōlua slide that extended over 200 feet down the southern slope. Unlike many other hōlua sled courses, this one was not paved and appears not to have had a platform. A long wooden sled was ridden down the prepared incline by ali'i in contests of courage and skill.

Nānāhoa Hill, now covered with ironwood trees, was once an active ancient site of great significance with its phallic rock, petroglyphs, and hōlua slide. A short distance from here is the Leina a ka 'Uhane, "leap of the soul," or jumping off place of the spirits of the dead. Now the area is part of Pālā'au State Park. There is a scenic overlook from the park, with a dramatic view of Kalaupapa peninsula 1,500 feet below. (6/94-95; 19/102; 21/48; 38/28-31)

13. **Kalaupapa (National Historical Park)**

Natural and archaeological features

(Wikimedia Commons)

Kalaupapa is an isolated, wind-swept peninsula lying below the towering cliffs of Moloka'i's mountainous north shore. Stretching at some points to over 2000 vertical feet, these sea cliffs are some of the highest in the world. The peninsula is divided into three ahupua'a (land divisions): Kalaupapa, Makanalua, and Kalawao. Kalaupapa means "much level land" and the peninsula is pretty much just that compared to the rest of the island. The region was formed well after the rest of the

LOCATION: On Moloka'i's isolated north shore, reached by air, by mule or by a three-mile hike (permit required).

island by lava flows from Kauhakō Crater, which rests prominently in the center of the peninsula. The name Kauhakō is said to refer to a mo'o, a lizard-like water creature that inhabited the small brackish lake inside the crater. The lake was once thought to be bottomless but, in fact, is about 814 feet deep and fluctuates with the tides. According to tradition, the volcano goddess Pele and her younger sister Hi'iaka created the crater by digging a hole in the peninsula. When water came up, extinguishing their volcanic fire, the sisters moved on to Maui. Two heiau and a hōlua slide are located on the crater, as is a small historic cemetary.

Kalaupapa is said to have been the favorite surfing spot of Moloka'i chiefs in ancient times. The surf here was called Pu'ao and the wind was Koki. Ever since 'Ai'ai, son of the fish god Kū'ula, left a fish stone on the peninsula, the area was blessed with an abundance of fish. The peninsula was also known as a bad-weather stopover for canoes traveling between Maui and O'ahu, and one of the many caves here showed occupation from at least a thousand years ago. There are many archaeological sites at Kalaupapa, including house sites, more than 16 heiau and shrines, birthing stones, a 750-foot hōlua slide, coastal ko'a, and dry land agricultural features. One heiau has an unusual upright stone foundation, constructed like a Tahitian marae (place of worship).

In 1865, the Hawaiian government (with the consent of King Kamehameha V) established Kalaupapa as a leper colony, a "place apart" for Hansen's disease victims, in an attempt to stem the spread of the feared disease. The 8,500-acre peninsula surrounded by rough water and abutting near-unscalable cliffs was a perfect quarantine area for the dread ma'i pākē (Chinese disease). The population of a small fishing village had to be relocated "topside." Hawaiians, with little immunity to introduced diseases, were easily susceptible to leprosy and one in fifty

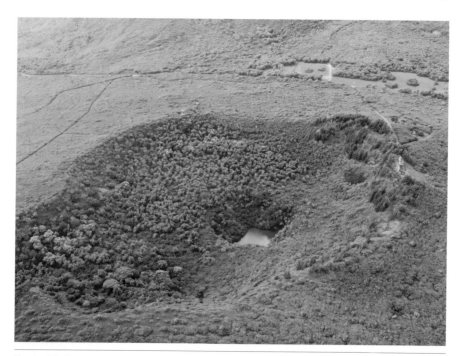

Kauhakō Crater sits prominently in the center of the peninsula and has a small brackish lake inside its overgrown cauldron that is 814 feet deep and fluctuates with the tides. A small cemetery, two heiau, and a hōlua slide are located on the crater.

Mokapu ("sacred district") and Okala ("bristling") Islets punctuate the north shore ocean just east of Kalaupapa.

contracted it. The worst cases were literally abandoned at Kalaupapa. Over the years, more than 8,000 people were sent here to die, and, at the height of the epidemic, over a thousand patients lived at the colony. In 1873, Joseph deVeuster, a Catholic priest known as Father Damien, arrived from Belgium to minister to the physical and spiritual needs of the Hansen's disease patients. Contracting the disease himself, he remained until his death in 1889 at age 49. For his remarkable care and treatment of the patients at Kalaupapa, Damien was canonized by the Catholic Church in 2009. Before his death he was joined by the Franciscan Sister Marianne Cope who was likewise canonized as a saint in 2012.

Today Kalaupapa is jointly administered by the State of Hawai'i Department of Health and the National Park Service. Kalaupapa became a national historical park in 1980. No new patients have been admitted since 1969 and only 8 patients still live, by choice, on the peninsula (at the time of this revised edition, 2016). Between 40 and 60 National Park workers and about 25 State employes are stationed here. The present-day Kalaupapa settlement is on the west side of the peninsula, but the original site of the colony was on the eastern end, known as Kalawao. It is here that Father Damien's church–dedicated to St. Philomena in 1872—stands surrounded by the graves of his parishioners and fellow workers. No one lives on the east side of the peninsula where the old settlement ruins are scattered about the dramatic coastal landscape.

Travel at Kalaupapa is tightly controlled in consideration of the patients' privacy; therefore, few ancient sites can be accessed. However, one can view a nameless heiau at the district boundary between

The historic St. Philomena Church, built in Honolulu and shipped to Kalaupapa in 1872, is the burial site of Saint Father Damien, although his body was later returned to his native Belgium and only the remains of one of his hands is buried here. There are only 1500 marked grave of the approximately 8000 Hansen disease patients buried at Kalaupapa.

the ahupua'a of Kalawao and Makanalua. Damien Tours, the only commercial operator of guided tours in the historic park, stops at the heiau where annual makahiki offerings, taxes for the district chiefs, were left in former times. There is a pā ahupua'a (boundary wall) that runs beside the temple and through the middle of the peninsula, except where it has been destroyed for the roadway. Further along the road, at Kalawao, the ruins of an ancient ko'a can be seen. If one stands in the graveyard of St. Philomena's Church and looks toward Mokapu ("sacred district") and Okala ("bristling") islets, one can just see the tops of a group of stones sticking up beyond the stone wall surrounding the church graveyard and abutting a field of unmarked graves. (There are over 6000 unmarked graves on the peninsula.) Across from the former site of the U.S. Leprosy Investigation Station, these stones, some upright, others strewn about, are the remains of the fishing shrine.

There was an ancient trail leading "topside" in the first valley to the east, Waihānau, before the present switchback trail was constructed into the colony. The former trail is now overgrown and inaccessible. There was also a simple but lengthy and effective irrigation system that Damien built from Waikolu Valley, adjacent to Mokapu and Okala Islets, all the way into the original settlement. Some of the stonework for this water system can be seen along the makai side of the road just west of the two churches in the old settlement.

Because of the displacement of its original population in order to create the Hansen's disease settlement in the nineteenth century, little oral tradition of pre-settlement times remains. However, because of the lack of development on the peninsula, Kalaupapa is an extremely valuable archaeological preserve. Eventually, under the guidance of the National Park Service, more of the ancient sites of Kalaupapa may become accessible to the public.

The most accessible heiau at Kalaupapa stands beside a pā ahupuaʻa, a boundary wall, that runs through the middle of the peninsula, and is where annual makahiki offerings, taxes for the district chiefs, were left.

Kalaupapa is jointly administered by the State of Hawai'i Department of Health and the National Park Service. Kalaupapa became a National Historical Park in 1980.

It is possible to visit Kalaupapa only by special arrangement with the National Parks Service or by taking one of the authorized local tours. Father Damien Tours at (808) 349-3006, www.fatherdamientours.com, provides information on Kalaupapa visits. Moloka'i Mule Ride at (800) 567-7550, www.muleride.com, arranges land access from Moloka'i "top side" and Makani Kai Air offers fly-in tours from Moloka'i Airport and from Honolulu, (808) 834-5813, www.makanikaiair.com. (19/98-123; 21/45; 32; 38/ 188-196)

> *Moloka'i 'āina o ka 'eha'eha.*
> Moloka'i, island of distress.
> [This expression came about after the establishment of the leper colony there. It refers to the separation of loved ones, the ravages of the disease, and the sad life in the early days at Kalawao, when so much was lacking for the comfort of the patients.] (31/238)
>
> —Hawaiian saying

ANCIENT SITES OF LĀNAʻI

Niniu Molokaʻi, poahi Lānaʻi.
Molokaʻi revolves, Lānaʻi sways.
[A description of the revolving of the hips and the swaying movements of the hula.] (31/252)
—Hawaiian saying

The papaya-shaped island of Lānaʻi lies 8 miles west of Maui and 9 miles south of Molokaʻi. Kahoʻolawe Island is 15 miles to the southeast and the four islands are arranged in such a way as to form a partially enclosed sea, a favored breeding ground of the humpback whale. Lānaʻi is a little more than 13 miles long and 13 miles wide, with its highest elevation at Lānaʻihale (Lānaʻi Hale), summiting at 3,379 feet. Lying in the lee of Maui and Molokaʻi, Lānaʻi receives little wave erosion on its northeast coast, but is often heavily battered from the southwest. Lānaʻi, like Kahoʻolawe, is drier than Maui and Molokaʻi being in their rain shadow, and it suffers from pronounced inland wind and rain erosion from the northeast.

According to chants from the time of Kamehameha, Wākea, the father of the Hawaiian Islands, took a new wife named Kaulawahine and she bore an island child, her first, called Lānaʻikaula. In another chant it was said that Lānaʻi was "found and adopted" from a Tahitian chief. Another form of the name Lānaʻi is Nānaʻi.

At one time, the gods Kāne and Kanaloa (two of the four major Hawaiian gods), together with their younger brother, Kāneʻāpua, lived at Kaunolū on Lānaʻi's southwest shore. They became thirsty, so Kāne and Kanaloa asked their younger brother to go upcountry to fetch water at a spring called Nānaʻihale (Lānaʻihale). After his long journey, Kāneʻāpua urinated into the spring before drawing water to take to his brothers. Upon his return to Kaunolū, Kāne and Kanaloa drank until their thirst was quenched only to realize they had drunk tainted water. They both fled from Lānaʻi, leaving Kāneʻāpua to fend for himself on Lānaʻi. It is said of Kāneʻāpua that he was a good navigator and knew how to read the stars and later went off on long distant voyages. The rock islet just off shore of Kaunolū is known as Lae o Kāneʻāpua.

Around 1400-1500, it is told that Lānaʻi was inhabited only by akua

Kāneʻāpua is the rock stack just off shore at Kaunolū and is named for the younger brother of the gods Kāne and Kanaloa.

(spirits) and for this reason no one would live on the island. In the old days, no one who visited Lānaʻi ever returned. Therefore, kapu breakers and wrongdoers were sent there as a punishment and as a death penalty for their crimes. Kaululāʻau, son of Maui chief Kakaʻalaneo, was sent to Lānaʻi as a punishment for pulling up so many breadfruit trees on Maui that the people of Lele (Lahaina) were in danger of going hungry. It was expected that he would be killed and eaten by the akua. However, while sleeping in a reed patch on his first night on the island, Kaululāʻau heard his ʻaumakua (guardian spirit) tell him to get up and go into a nearby cave to sleep. The next day the spirits asked him where he had slept and he replied: "In the reed patch." The spirits were baffled over why they had not found him there. They asked him where he would sleep the next night and he replied: "In the high crashing surf." Those spirits that looked for him there were battered by the surf and carried away by the strong ocean currents. Kaululāʻau then built a hale (house) on the highest point of Lānaʻi, Lānaʻihale, and once again tricked the spirits into thinking he was sleeping there. When they entered he set the hut on fire and did away with the bad akua. And so it went with Kaululāʻau deceiving the spirits until even the chief spirit was vanquished from the island. During his stay on Lā-

Lānaʻi's highest mountain, at an elevation of 3,379 feet, is Lānaʻihale (Lānaʻi Hale), "house of the day of conquest." It is a wahi pana of the triumphant human spirit and the site of an ancient heiau. (Wikimedia Commons)

na'i, Kaululā'au kept a fire lit so that all would know on Maui that the chief's son was still alive. Eventually, a canoe was sent to bring him home, where he returned to a hero's welcome for making Lāna'i ("day [of] conquest") livable. Thus the epithet: Lāna'i o Kaululā'au.

Another tradition concerns Kawelo, the great kahuna of Lāna'i who kept a sacred fire burning at a location known as Keahiakawelo. He was a rival of the Moloka'i kahuna Lanikaula ("divine prophet"). Kawelo went to Moloka'i in order to defeat Lanikaula by stealing his excrement and burning it on his fire. Lanikaula knew he would die when he saw the smoke from Kawelo's fire (Lāna'i site 1, Moloka'i site 2). According to legend, Kawelo later threw himself off the cliffs at Maunalei and killed himself.

Later, under the rule of Maui Chief Pi'ilani, Lāna'i flourished for some time. It was during this period that Lāna'i was probably divided into its 13 ahupua'a or land districts, which are still acknowledged today. When Captain James Cook's ships replenished their supplies along Lāna'i's windward coast in 1778, he noted it was a dustbowl but estimated a population of 10,000 based on conversations with informants. Less than a year after Cook's visit, the Hawai'i Island chief Kalaniopu'u and his army went into war against their neighbors. The chief had been forced to retreat from a campaign against Lahaina, Maui. He stopped at Kaho'olawe, where his army massacred the entire population. Then, encouraged by his victory against this small island of commoners, Kalaniopu'u and his war-

riors returned to Lahaina, where they were defeated a second time. Fleeing Maui, the enraged army set upon Lāna'i where it systematically destroyed all the villages. Kalaniopu'u returned to the Big Island after yet another unsuccessful campaign against central Maui, where he died within the year, leaving the struggle for interisland domination to his nephew

Kawelo, the great 16th century kahuna of Lāna'i, kept a sacred fire burning at a location known as Keahiakawelo ("the fire of Kawelo"), more recently called the Garden of the Gods. His fire could be seen on Moloka'i across the channel.

Kamehameha. In 1795, Kamehameha the Great took all the Hawaiian Islands, with the exception of Kaua'i.

In the 1800s, the Native Hawaiian population began to diminish at a rapid rate due to lack of immunity to common illnesses brought in by foreigners. In the mid-1800s, the Ka'a area in sparsely populated Lāna'i was used as a penal colony for women, just as the island of Kaho'olawe was similarly used for men. The population of Lāna'i remained small with only a minor growth spurt between 1854 and 1864 when the Mormon Church established a mission on the island and again between 1899 and 1901 when the Maunalei Sugar Company was being developed. Both endeavours failed and only about 120 people were living on Lāna'i by the early twentieth century. Estimates put the island's population at 6,000 at the end of the 1700s and at approximately half that by the 1820s. Today's population has remained steady for the last half century at around 3,000 residents.

It wasn't until pineapple was introduced in the 1920s that the population increased due to immigrant labor being brought in, mostly from the Philippines. In 1922, James Dole purchased most of the island and as president of the Hawaiian Pineapple Company (later the Dole Food Company) established the world's largest pineapple plantation. It is for this reason that Lāna'i is referred to as the Pineapple Island. In 1959 when Hawai'i became a state, Lāna'i became part of Maui County. In 1985, David Murdock took control of the Dole land holdings through his purchase of its owner Castle & Cooke. Pineapple was eventually phased out in the 1990s after 70 years of operation and 16,000 acres of cultivation. Today, tourism is the mainstay of the island.

Billionaire Larry Ellison, founder of Oracle Corporation, bought approximately 98% of the island (the state and private land holders own the other 2%) in 2012 for an estimated $500+ million. He has pledged that at least

Although there are many ancient sites on the island (23 petroglyph sites, more than 10 large heiau, numerous small shrines and ko'a, house and burial sites, several fishpond ruins and ancient trails), only some of these are accessible at the present time. This heiau, the largest on the island, measuring 55 feet wide by 152 feet long is not easily accessible. It is at Ka'ena Iki ("the little point of heat") and is in an area of village ruins and agricultural terraces. (Photo by Kepā Maly)

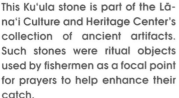

This Ku'ula stone is part of the Lāna'i Culture and Heritage Center's collection of ancient artifacts. Such stones were ritual objects used by fishermen as a focal point for prayers to help enhance their catch.

The Lāna'i Culture and Heritage Center, located in the center of Lāna'i City, was established in order to initiate preservation efforts and to educate residents and visitors about the cultural sites and history of Lāna'i Island.

that amount more of investment will go toward establishing Lāna'i as an eco-friendly, self-sustainable and livably healthy island. The Pūlama Lāna'i holding company was formed to meet this goal.

Interest in Lāna'i's ancient cultural and archaeological sites has grown in recent years. The Lāna'i Culture and Heritage Center was established and together with Pūlama Lāna'i, and the people of Lāna'i is keen on protecting and even featuring these sites. Although there are many ancient sites on the island (23 petroglyph sites, more than 10 large heiau, numerous small shrines and ko'a, house and burial sites, several fishpond ruins and ancient trails that are known), only some of these are accessible at the present time. Accessibility of some sites should be confirmed with Pūlama Lāna'i (565-3000) or the Lāna'i Culture and Heritage Center (565-7177). The sites mentioned in these pages give a rich and rewarding impression of Lāna'i's ancient past and the smartphone app Lāna'i Guide also provides useful information on these and other historic sites. (6; 9/11-14; 12; 20/132-135; 26; 29)

> *I puni ia 'oe o Lāna'i a i 'ike 'ole ia Lāna'i-Ka'ula me Lāna'i-Hale, 'a'ohe no 'oe i 'ike ia Lāna'i.*
> If you have gone around Lāna'i and have not seen Lāna'i Ka'ula and Lāna'ihale, you have not seen all of Lāna'i.
> (31/1258)
>
> —Hawaiian saying

Lāna'i Site Map

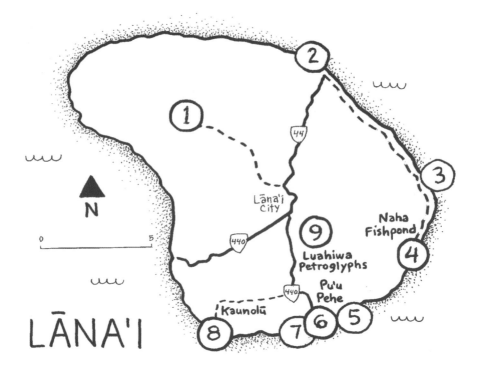

Lāna'i Site List

1. Keahiakawelo (Garden of the Gods)
2. Pō'āiwa Petroglyphs
3. Waia'ōpae Fishpond
4. Naha Fishpond and Trail
5. Pu'u Pehe (Sweetheart Rock)
6. Hulopo'e
7. Kapiha'a Village Interpretive Trail
8. Kaunolū
9. Luahiwa Petroglyphs

I. Keahiakawelo (Garden of the Gods)

Natural area with numerous boulders

Popularly known as the Garden of the Gods, in part, because of its unearthly landscape and otherworldly rock formations (it was given this name in 1912 when a travel writer compared it to the Garden of the Gods canyon in Colorado), Keahiakawelo (Keahi a Kawelo), is the ancient site of "the fire of Kawelo." In this large land district of Ka'a, with its clear view of Moloka'i, there are numerous large ahu (piled stones) and boulders, one of which is said to be the altar of the Lāna'i kahuna, Kawelo. He lived some

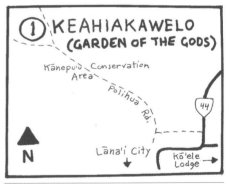

LOCATION: **Six and a half miles northwest of Lāna'i City along unpaved Polihua Road. Follow signs and cross two animal guards. Do not park on the roadway.**

three generations before the great Maui chief Kahekili and he kept a constant fire burning upon his altar.

In one story, Kawelo noticed some of the people of Lāna'i seemed to be under a supernatural spell. He determined that Lanikaula, the Moloka'i kahuna, was to blame. Pretending to be a friend, Kawelo went to Moloka'i and stayed with Lanikaula and his three sons at Hālawa,

Popularly known as the Garden of the Gods because of its otherworldly rock formations, Keahiakawelo, or Keahi a Kawelo, is the ancient site of "the fire of Kawelo."

where he hoped to discover the secret place where Lanikaula disposed
of his excrement. By burning the rival kahuna's kūkae (excrement),
Kawelo would be able to carry out the lawe maunu ceremony and pray
his victim to death. But Kawelo had little luck in discovering Lanikaula's kapu place until one night he managed to get his host drunk with
'awa. Then Kawelo saw that Lanikaula went to a small offshore rock islet
to do his business. When Lanikaula fell asleep, Kawelo stole his host's
canoe, crossed to the rock island, collected the needed material, hiding
it in a hollowed out sweet potato, and returned to Lāna'i. When Lanikaula awoke and looked across the channel, he saw the fire of Kawelo
burning brightly and he knew from the dark purple color and shape of
the smoke that he was going to die. (Legend tells that the lehua blos-
soms in this area of Lāna'i turned purple from the smoke.) He asked
his three sons where they would hide his bones when he died to keep
them safe from his enemies, and his oldest son said he would throw
them into the deep ocean where no one could find them. But Lanikaula
said that would not be satisfactory, and he asked the second son, who
said he would throw them off a high cliff to where none could find them.
But again, Lanikaula said that would not keep his bones safe. He then
asked the youngest, who replied that he would dig a pit for the bones
and cover them with stones. To this the kahuna answered that his
remains would be well hidden. It is believed that Lanikaula is buried
in the sacred kukui grove, Ulukukui o Lanikaula, at Pu'u Hōkū (see
Moloka'i site 2).

A further story tells of Kawelo's daughter who helped him stoke the
sacred fire. It was said that, as long as the fire burned, the island would
have an abundant supply of pigs and dogs. Over on Moloka'i lived the

kahuna Waha, whose son assisted him in maintaining a similar sacred fire. Waha's son, Nui, loved Kawelo's daughter, Pepe, and would often visit her by paddling across the channel to Lāna'i in his canoe. One night the two lovers spent so long in each other's company that they let both fires go out. Fearing the wrath of their fathers, they fled to Maui. In anguish, Kawelo threw himself off the pali (cliff) at Maunalei, and it is said that the people of Lāna'i believe that the extinction of their native swine and canines was due to the poor tending of Kawelo's fire.

It has become a custom for visitors to the Keahiakawelo to build rock altars in the open, windswept landscape by stacking piles of stones one upon another. The stone ahu represents the kūkae (excrement) of Lanikaula, offered up by Kawelo in order to pray the Moloka'i kahuna to death. This practice of stacking stones is discouraged today.

To reach Keahiakawelo one passes through Kānepu'u Preserve, managed by The Nature Conservancy of Hawai'i for the protection of rare and endangered plants. Here live 48 native species, including dryland nā'ū (Hawaiian gardenia), Lāna'i sandalwood, and regional persimmon. Kānepu'u (Kāne Hill) is the name of the highest elevation in this area (1,799 feet), just to the south of the Garden of the Gods. (9/18-19; 12; 26)

2. Pō'āiwa Petroglyphs

Rock carvings

The Pō'āiwa Petroglyphs (also referred to as the Kukui Point Petroglyphs) are on a basalt rock outcropping beside a dry gulch in the Mahana land district of northern Lāna'i, an area that receives less than 10 inches of rain a year. The site lies about 200 yards uphill from the beach, and is covered with kiawe trees, not the kukui (candlenut) trees one would expect from the place name of Kukui Point. Little is known of the surrounding area just inland from what is today referred to as Shipwreck Beach. (Two US Navy ships were intentionally run aground along this coastline following WWII.) However, with its clear views of and direct proximity to Maui and Moloka'i it would have recieved some interisland traffic as well as local seasonal visitation in ancient times.

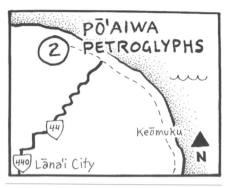

LOCATION: **Take Keōmoku Road north out of Lāna'i City, about 8.3 miles to where the pavement ends. Turn left on the sandy road (only if you have four-wheel drive) and go 1.5 miles to the end of the track. Continue uphill on foot, following the signage and stone ahu. The petroglyph outcrop lies just a few yards beyond a large boulder that reads "Do Not Deface."**

In this area there are about 85 images that include human figures, birdmen, dogs and birds. The longer one looks for petroglyphs here, the more the images reveal themselves. It takes some time to sensitize one's eyes to the subtly carved images that are most easily seen in early morning or late afternoon when the sun is low.

Kenneth Emory, one of the first archaeologists to survey Lāna'i in the early 1920s, noted that ki'i pōhaku (petroglyphs) of animals and

A marked trail leads to the Pō'āiwa Petroglyph site. Follow the signage and stacked stone ahu. The petroglyph outcrop lies just a few yards beyond a large boulder that ironically reads "Do Not Deface."

There are said to be about 85 pecked or abraded petroglyph images in this area that include human figures, birdmen, birds and dogs. Human figures appear here in both the stick figure and the triangular body type.

humans were located near small village sites and along trails on Lāna'i. He said the images were done over generations and were similar to those found on other Hawaiian Islands, but "the dog was the most common of animal forms represented." There is even a dog on a leash being led by a human figure. Human figures appear here at Pō'āiwa in both the stick figure and the triangular body type.

Four other petroglyph sites are in the region with less than 50 images in total. These are difficult to find and off the beaten path. Please protect the petroglyphs by not marking on or around them. Photographing is best in the early morning or late afternoon. (6/90-91; 9)

3. Waia'ōpae Fishpond

Fishpond ruins

This ancient fishpond, long since destroyed, is now under reconstruction with the help of local community groups. There are also numerous heiau and some petroglyph sites in this area, but they are not easily accessible or have been destroyed. Their presence indicates that this was a frequented area in ancient times.

An interesting telling of the story of Kaululā'au, son of Maui Chief Kaka'alaneo, was that when he was sent to Lāna'i as a punishment for pulling up his father's breadfruit trees and it was expected that he would be killed by the bad akua (spirits), he actually got the demon spirits to work for him, plowing fields and building fishponds. In this way it is said that Kaululā'au made the island livable and people began to settle here because of the plentiful crops and good fishing. In this telling, Kaululā'au stays on Lāna'i until his father comes to see if the tales of his son and the island's transformation are true. Chief Kaka'alaneo is pleased to see that Kaululā'au has become a wise and generous leader to the people of Lāna'i and has left his wayward behavior behind. Waia'ōpae Fishpond may have been one of the construction projects Kaululā'au made the akua perform.

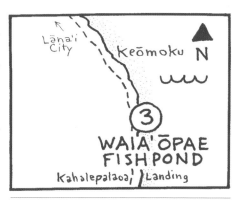

LOCATION: **Along the coastal 4-wheel drive dirt road, 6 miles from paved Keōmoku Road, route 44, and just past Keōmoku Village.**

In 1829, Queen Ka'ahumanu, nearly 70 years old, came to Kahalepalaoa and preached to the people of Lāna'i that they might convert to Christianity. Kahalepalaoa means "the storehouse of ivory," and it was along this coastal region that beached whales left behind their precious bones. Later, the Maunalei Sugar Company was established in this area for a very brief time and a population of nearly 2,000 lived in and around Keōmoku. However, it is said that things started to go wrong when stones from a nearby heiau were used to build the bed of a 6-mile long, narrow-gage train track for hauling sugar to Kahalepalaoa Landing. Japanese field workers fell sick and died. A drought struck and precious spring water turned brackish and became undrinkable. Maunalei Sugar Company went bankrupt in 1901 after only a brief time in operation. The population of Lāna'i dwindled to about 100 in the early years of the twentieth century, only 50 living around Keōmoku. An historic wooden building, Ka Lanakila Church, now renovated, together with an old stone ruin, Kahalepalaoa Church, a rusted cane haul train, a Japanese burial site and shrine, and a few other features from more recent times are all that remain of this ghost township of eastern Lāna'i. Ancient heiau and petroglyphs were also in this area but are mostly destroyed.

Native Hawaiian scholar Samuel Kamakau stated that: "Fishponds, loko i'a, were things that beautified the land, and a land with many fishponds was called "fat" land ('aina momona). They date from very ancient times."

Gradually being restored, the Waia'ōpae Fishpond, between Keōmoku and Kahalepalaoa Landing is one of four ancient pond ruins along this windward coastline. The others are Ka'a Loko, Kahōkeo and Naha Fishpond (site 4). It is located in the ahupua'a of Pālāwai ("fresh water moss") that stretches right across the island and includes the

highest peak of Lāna'ihale. In 1854, during the Māhele when land claims were established, the ahupua'a was awarded to Chiefess Kekau'ōnohi and her husband Ha'alelea. At this time 'anae (mullet) was a kapu fish.

The original pond was 2000 feet long and went a distance of 571 feet out into the ocean, enclosing 9 acres of shoreline. At the time of this writing a substantial section of the kuapā was completed by community volunteer efforts. Only rocks and natural resources from the immediate vicinity are used in the construction and all work is done by hand, no mechanized equipment is used. Close monitoring of water quality, endangered species, and archaeological features is carried out at the site.

The historic wooden Ka Lanakila Church, now renovated, is one of the few reminders of the former activity in this area between Keōmoku Village and Kahalepalaoa Landing. Kahalepalaoa Church ruin, perhaps the first stone and mortar building on Lāna'i, was constructed in 1837. A Japanese burial site and other historic features are all that remain of this once booming area of the island. Japanese kanji inscribed on an upright burial shrine stone symbolize the three realms of transmigration of the soul after death: the Realm of Desire, the Realm of Forms, and the Realm of Formlessness.

Waiaʻōpae Fishpond was 2000 feet long and went a distance of 571 feet out into the ocean enclosing 9 acres of coastal waters.

The Lānaʻi Culture and Heritage Center coordinates regular workdays throughout the year. (9/64; 41)

4. Naha Fishpond and Trail

Fishpond ruins and trail

Naha (meaning "curved" or "bent") is the name of a valley, a fishpond, a trail and former village site on southeastern Lānaʻi. At the very end of the dirt road, just visible along the shoreline and dotted out into the ocean, is the ancient ruin of Naha Fishpond, visible at low tide. Along the eastern coastline of Lānaʻi were several fishponds, specifically at Lōpā and near Keōmoku (Waiaʻōpae, Kahōkeo and Kaʻa Loko). However, most of these have been destroyed, with the exception of the partially restored Waia'ōpae Fishpond (see site 3).

Fishponds were built by order of the local or visiting high chiefs. Some pondcatch was entirely reserved for ali'i, while others were available to the whole community. It was kapu for menstruating women to walk on the pond walls for fear of defiling the kuapā and the loko i'a. A kahuna 'aumakua ho'oulu i'a loko kuapā was necessary to choose the proper wood for the mākāhā, sluice gates, usually 'ohi'a or lama wood. About five or

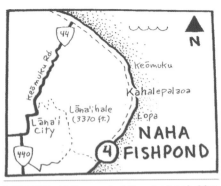

LOCATION: **At the end of the 4-wheel drive coastal dirt road, 12 miles from paved Keōmoku Road, route 44. Be sure to have water if you venture out this far. There are no services whatsoever.**

six months after the completion of a fishpond the fish would begin to be seen (aholehole, awa'aua, kaku, 'o'opu-hue, 'o'opu, and the 'opae). Fish would congregate and feed at the pond gates where salty seawater and fresh sweetwater would mingle in a nutrient rich, brackish mixture.

An ancient heiau was on the ridge above the fishpond and a paved trail begins here ascending the lower slopes of 3,370-foot Lāna'ihale, the highest elevation on the island. The rough trail most likely follows an even older path to the uplands but the stone paving was likely laid down in the 1840s by order of the governor of Maui, Chief Hoapili. Male prison laborers from Kaho'olawa were probably used to carry out the work. Kaho'olawa is the now uninhabited, low-lying island that sits directly across the channel to the east. A good view of the Naha Fishpond ruins is afforded from the upper elevations of the Naha Trail. A heiau site is also on the hill above Naha. (9; 41)

An ancient paved trail begins just above Naha Fishpond and ascends the lower slopes of Lāna'ihale, the highest mountain on the island. A good view of Naha Fishpond is afforded from the upper elevations of the Naha Trail.

5. **Pu'u Pehe**

Offshore island and shrine

It is said that Pu'u Pehe was the daughter of Uaua, a Maui chief, and she was captured as a war prize by the young ali'i Maka-kēhau of Lāna'i. Makakēhau was called, "Misty Eyes," because the beauty of Pu'u Pehe had blinded him and made him hide his love prize away in isolated places, afraid that he might lose her. One day he left her in the sea cave of Malauea to prepare food, while he went to the mountain spring of Pūlo'u to collect sweetwater in his gourd. From the uplands he noticed the front of a Kona storm

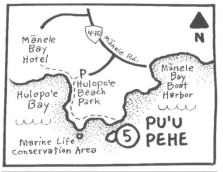

LOCATION: **Eight miles south of Lāna'i City at the end of Route 440 (Mānele Road), and a quarter mile hike on a coastal track from the Hulopo'e Beach Park parking lot.**

approaching the island. He ran down the slope as fast as he could to warn his wife, but high surf had crashed into the cave and drowned her before he could reach his beloved. Helped by the gods, he recovered her body and carried it to the top of a small rock islet under cover of night. By morning he had finished preparing a grave for his loved one on the islet's summit. After placing the last stone as an upright marker, he stood and cried out:

Where are you, o Pu'u Pehe?
Are you in the cave of Malauea?
Shall I bring you sweet water?
Shall we dip in the gourd together?
The bird and fish are bitter
And the mountain water is sour.
I shall drink it no more;
I shall drink it with 'Aipuhi,
The great shark of Mānele.(9/72)

Makakēhau ceased his lament and, before the eyes of those watching from the nearby shore cliffs, he threw himself into the crashing breakers below.

On the summit of Pu'u Pehe is a stone platform 6 feet wide and 3 feet high. An 18-inch tall, 8-inch square stone is set upright in the northern section of the platform. The platform, with its longer axis directed to the northwest is in the center of the islet's summit.

Today, the small rock islet where the beautiful maiden is said to be buried is within Mānele-Hulopo'e Marine Life Conservation Area and is called Pu'u Pehe. The 1.1-acre sea tower stands 80 feet high and is 60 feet from the southern coastal pali of Hulopo'e Park at Mānele. The cave of Malauea is at the base of the cliff at the west edge of the small bay facing Pu'u Pehe.

No human remains have been discovered in the 2 inches of soil above bedrock on Pu'u Pehe. But the numerous bird bones, mostly tern, and shells led one archaeologist to speculate that the shrine might be a bird ko'a used in ritual practice by bird hunters. One translation of Pu'u Pehe is "Owl Trap Hill." Hawaiian historian Kamakau tells us: "The bird islands and the people who caught birds by trapping, smoking, and striking had ko'a to sustain the land with plenty of birds." Pu'u Pehe may well have been such a bird shrine, sacred to ancient Hawaiian bird hunters.

Between May and November the 'ua'u kani (Hawaiian Wedgetailed Shearwater) migrates thousands of miles to the Mānele-Hulopo'e sand dunes in order to mate and care for their young. A single egg is buried in the sand and watched over in shifts by the parents. After 50 days the hatchling is watched over for another week then left on its own to fend for itself. Numbers of the rare bird have diminished over the year. Please be aware of their presence in the area.

Today, Pu'u Pehe is often called Sweetheart Rock. (9/72-73; 12/55)

6. **Hulopo'e**

Ancient village ruins

The sparse remains of an ancient fishing village can be found at the righthand, northern end of Hulopo'e Beach. Just below the Four Seasons Resort, low lying rock walls indicate the former house sites, canoe shed foundations, and other archaeological features that are part of the Hulopo'e Heritage Trail. Interpretive signs describe many of the site features and detail aspects of ancient Hawaiian village life. Display maps make clear the layout of what foundation stones of the

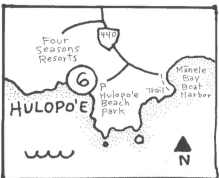

LOCATION: **Eight miles south of Lāna'i City at the end of Route 440 (Mānele Road), and on the Four Season Resort side of Hulopo'e Beach.**

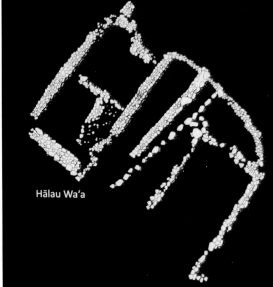

Hālau Wa'a

ancient village can still be seen.

Hulopo'e was probably first used as a fishermen's campsite about 800 years ago. Gradually a permanent settlement was established leaving only these house site foundation stones. The people of this village were part of the ahupua'a of Pālāwai which stretched across the uplands of the island and over to the windward coast; an unusually extensive land division. This made for good trading of island-wide resources.

Hawaiian historian, Samuel Kamakau, pointed out the importance of agriculture and fishing in ancient Hawai'i: "The Hawaiian people were a race of expert fishermen. The art had been handed down from their ancestors. Agriculture and fishing were the two main professions always passed

Just below the Four Seasons Resort and at the northern end of Hulopo'e Beach, low lying rock walls indicate the former hale (house) sites, hālau wa'a (canoe shed) foundations, and other archaeological features that are part of the Hulopo'e Heritage Trail. Interpretive signs describe many of the sites and detail aspects of ancient Hawaiian village life.

Hulopoʻe Heritage Trail leads along the coast and away from the beach and turns into the Kapihaʻā Village Interpretive Trail, going on to an adjacent village site to the west.

on by the grandparents to the grandchildren." Trade between the coastal fishing and upland farming communities guaranteed a balance diet of fish and seafood, and taro and sweet potato.

From the 1860s to the 1920s, ranching was the main commercial activity on Lānaʻi. First sheep and goats, later cattle, were the primary stock in trade. Cattle ("pipi" in Hawaiian) were originally kapu as a royal animal that had been gifted by foreign interests. They propagated quickly throughout the islands and eventually required control by means of ranching. In the early 20th century, the Lānaʻi Ranch would drive their pipi into the ocean at Manele Bay and load them on to ships for market. Later, a chute was built on the Leinohaunui Cliffs beside Manele Boat Harbor. A short fishermen's trail on the righthand, south side of the harbor leads up to where the Pipi Chute was located. In the 1930s, mortar salt making beds were built at the harbor and later moved to the top of the cliffs. The saltpans were regularly filled with salt water that evaporated in the sun and left just the salt, a practice the ancient Hawaiians had done for centuries.

Back at Hulopoʻe Beach, a trail leading along the coast and away from the beach takes one to the Kapihaʻā Village Interpretive Trail, an adjacent village site, about a quarter-mile to the west. The ancient sites along Hulopoʻe Heritage Trail and the Kapihaʻā Village Interpretive Trail are protected by State Law. However, it is up to visitors to not disturb any of the rock features in these areas and to stay on the trail. (9; 12; 16)

7. Kapiha'ā Village Interpretive Trail

Village ruins, heiau and trail

The Kapiha'ā Village Interpretive Trail can be accessed from two different points and runs about a half-mile through the ancient ruins of this leeward Lāna'i former fishing village. The trail can be entered from Hulopo'e Heritage Trail that begins at Hulopo'e Beach Park or it can be started from the Challenge Golf Clubhouse at the end of Challenge Drive. The Kapiha'ā Archaeological Preserve contains no less than fifteen distinctive sites with at least 60 distinguishable features including house sites, ceremonial sites, agricultural fields, and lithic workshops. The area was probably first settled around 800 years ago.

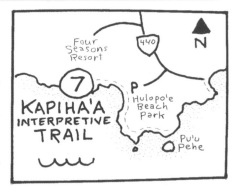

LOCATION: **Eight miles south of Lāna'i City near the end of Route 440 (Mānele Road). Turn right on Hulopo'e Road and left on Challenge Drive to get to the Challenge Golf Club House. Just below the clubhouse signs mark the trailhead. The coastal track may also be accessed from Hulopo'e Beach Park via Hulopo'e Heritage Trail. See Hulopo'e (site 6).**

Numbered signage begins the trail route just below the golf clubhouse. From here there is a panoramic view of Hulopo'e-Mānele Bay and Pu'u Pehe Islet. Following the trail to sign 4, one encounters a ceremonial site, a heiau. This heiau includes a walled platform measuring 35 feet by 42 feet with some walls standing 4 to 6 feet high. The interior is paved with boulders and some exposed bedrock. The size and situation of this ritual site suggests that it was a heiau dedicated to the gods of fishing and/or agriculture, perhaps even a rain deity. Please stay on the trail and don't move rocks or walk on archaeological features.

The Kapiha'ā heiau includes a walled platform measuring 35 feet by 42 feet with some walls standing 4 to 6 feet high.

As one proceeds along the trail, natural agricultural terraces come into view. The dryland agriculture of former times could have produced here 'uala (sweet potato), uhi (yams), hue (gourds), ki (ti), and kō (sugarcane). The two villages of Kapiha'ā and Hulopo'e-Mānele could have supported a population of serveral hundred people at one time. Some of the habitation sites were likely used only seasonally.

Near sign 6 you will notice house sites with multiple terraces, each level dedicated to a different domestic function. Scattered seashells, basalt flakes, and coral can be seen, remnants of food consumption and tool making over many generations. Please do not pick up or take anything from the preserve.

From sign 7 a ko'a or fishing shrine can be seen to the west. Portions of this site have collapsed but the upright stone on a foundation full of coral makes it clear that this was an altar to the god Kū'ula, the god of fishermen. Seeking protection and good luck, fishermen would make an offering to Ku'ulakai (male) or Hinapukui'a (female) at such ko'a sites and on return would offer some of their catch and gratitude. Fishery resources in the area would have included limu (seaweed), pāpa'i (crabs), pūpū (shellfish), he'e (octopus), and wana (urchins) in addition to the many varieties of fish. Fishermen also used ko'a to triangulate their location and find specific fishing grounds. By lining up a ko'a and other natural landmarks a fisherman could identify select offshore fishing spots.

The Kapiha'ā Village Interpretive Trail is along an ancient ala hele (trail) that connected coastal villages in the area and had branches that

ran to the uplands. Like the Naha Trail (site 4), this ala hele was important as a trade route and thoroughfare that connected families and villages. Work on this trail was organized by the Lāna'i Culture and Heritage Center and supported by many local groups and State organizations. For additional information contact the LCHC. 730 Lāna'i Avenue, Suite 118, Lāna'i City, HI 96763, Phone: (808) 565-7177, www.lanaichc.org (9; 12; 16)

The Kapiha'ā Village Interpretive Trail runs along an ancient ala hele (trail) that connected coastal villages in the area and had auxiliary trails that ran to the uplands. Views of Kaho'olawe and Maui are possible on clear days.

8. **Kaunolū**

Ancient village ruins, heiau, petroglyphs

It is said that he gods Kāne and Kanaloa lived at Kaunolū for a time, together with their younger brother Kāne'āpua. Kāne and Kanaloa sent their sibling to fetch water at an upcountry spring called Nāna'ihale (Lāna'ihale). Unfortunately, Kāne'āpua relieved himself in the spring before collecting water to take back to his brothers. Upon his return to Kaunolū, Kāne and Kanaloa drank the water to quench their thirst only to realize they had drunk polluted water. They both departed Lāna'i in disgust, leaving Kāne'āpua to fend for himself. The rock island just off shore of Kaunolū is called Kāne'āpua.

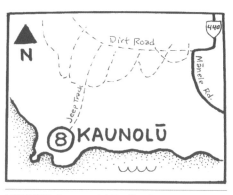

LOCATION: Proceed 4.5 miles from Lāna'i City along Manele Road, route 440. Shortly after the sharp lefthand turn make a right turn at the 10-mile marker on to a dirt road and proceed 2.6 miles to the Hawaiian warrior sign. Turn left and head downhill 3.3 miles. This drive requires a 4-wheel drive vehicle.

The rock stack just off shore from Kaunolū is known as Kāne'āpua, named for the younger brother of the gods Kāne and Kanaloa. Above Kāne'āpua and on the westside of Kaunolū Gulch is Halulu Heiau, which served as a pu'uhonua for kapu breakers. Kamehameha apparently held ceremonies here between 1778 and 1810.

The village ruins of Kaunolū exhibit the distinctive wahi pana of a once-active fishing community abandoned well over a hundred years ago. Ohua, the last resident and son of the district konohiki (caretaker), died here around 1900. He is said to have been told by Kamehameha V in 1868 to hide the stone image of the fish god, Kūnihi, which stood upon a stone altar below the heiau. His mishandling of the image is reputed to have caused his death.

Archaeological surveys in 1921 and 1991 established the village as consisting of 86 house platforms, 35 rock shelters, and 30 detached enclosures. The ruins straddle a dry gulch and overlook a small bay. One of the house sites is believed to be where Kamehameha the Great, as a young man, resided when he visited Lāna'i with his elders from the island of Hawai'i to engage in deep-sea fishing.

The remains of a canoe shelter can be seen at the water's edge in Kaunolū. Kūnihi was one of the major deities worshiped here seasonally by fishermen. Kahekili's Leap is a lele kawa (cliff jumping) place with a sheer drop to the sea below. It is named for the Maui Chief Kahekili, who practiced cliff jumping in various places throughout Hawai'i. It is also said to be a leina a ka 'uhane ("leaping place of the spirit") where souls of the dead would jump into the next world. Petroglyphs at Kaunolū depict birdmen, a theme found on other Hawaiian Islands and throughout the Pacific region.

On the westside of Kaunolū Gulch is Halulu Heiau, which served as a pu'uhonua for the redemption of kapu breakers but also had a precinct that was a luakini heiau for human sacrifice. Halulu was a Bird Man and companion of the god Kāne. His name and spirit were called on by cliff jumpers to assist their leaps from great heights, and by high chiefs and kāhuna wishing to expand their kingdoms. The temple was dedicated to this sacred bird god and Kamehameha the Great

Many cultural sites around the Hawaiian Islands are marked with the crowned and caped ali'i warrior sign as is Kaunolū.

evidently held ceremonies here at Halulu Heiau between 1778 and 1810, calling on this god to help him in his bid for uniting the Hawaiian Islands. The heiau measures 50 feet by 120 feet in its present configuration and has three terrace levels, each a foot higher than the other.

At the top of the hill behind the heiau is Kahekili's Leap, a breathtaking spot at the edge of a cliff overlooking the sea below, where lele kawa (cliff jumping) was practiced. Maui chief Kahekili was known for his practice of this extreme sport, during which he challenged his warriors to display their courage, calling on Halulu the bird god, and following their chief over the cliff and into the water below. It was also said that kapu breakers would be sentenced to jump off here and if innocent they would survive the fall. It is also believed to be one of the leina a ka 'uhane, "leaping places of the spirits," where souls of the dead pass over into the other world, the realm of Pō. (The World Cliff Diving Championship took place here in 2001.)

Ko'a (fishing shrines), a hālau wa'a (canoe house), and petroglyphs are also found at this dramatic natural site (note the Bird Man petroglyphs).

On the eastside of the gulch is Keālia Kapu-Kaunolū Heritage Complex, the boundary area between Keālia Kapu and Kaunolū, two of the thirteen ahupua'a of Lāna'i. This is an exceptional wahi pana with features such as Kamehameha I house site, an ancient kōnane game stone (something like a checkerboard), petroglyphs, an ancient trail and other points of interest. Signage gives descriptions of the various site features. Do not cross the gulch if the stream is flowing. (9/51-60; 21/58-59)

9. **Luahiwa Petroglyphs**

Rock carvings

Although Lāna'i is one of the smaller of the Hawaiian Islands, it has numerous and widely distributed examples of petroglyphs. Many forms, mostly human and animal, are carved on lava boulders and cliffs, at village and coastal sites such as Kaunolū

LOCATION: Due to erosion of the hillside at the Luahiwa Petroglyphs conservation efforts are presently limiting access to the site in order to better preserve it. In future it may be that a proper viewing platform is constructed to best feature this exceptional site.

and Kukui, as well as at upland locations such Luahiwa. Two-dozen sites in all have been located on Lāna'i.

The Luahiwa site is on the lower slopes of a ridge that rises out of the fertile volcanic soil of Pālāwai Basin to summit at 3,370-foot Lāna'ihale. In the early twentieth century the basin was the home of the largest pineapple plantation in the world, but in ancient times it was a productive area for growing Hawaiian sweet potatoes. In the mid-1800s a Mormon settlement was active in the Pālāwai Basin.

The Luahiwa ("sacred black pit") Petroglyphs are carved on 20 boulders, some of which are arranged in a semicircle, and are found spread over a sloping area of three acres. The site is on the boundary between the ahupua'a (land division) of Keāliaaupuni ("the salt pans of the government") and Keāliakapu ("the sacred salt pans") and contains about 400 individual images. The carvings represent the most varied petroglyphs on the island, in terms of theme, as well as in estimated

With some four hundred petroglyphs on twenty boulders, Luahiwa is the richest of the twenty-three petroglyph sites on Lāna'i. This boulder features human figures, horses and riders (horses were introduced in 1804), and dogs (some on leashes).

age range. Newer images appear to be carved beside and overlapping older ones. Early triangular-bodied human figures are sometimes overlapped with later post-contact images, such as a horse with rider, a figure with a gun, a deer, dogs with curly tails, and letters of the alphabet.

There are also remains of what has been described as a rain heiau used for the purpose of calling forth light showers and cloud bursts. (6/90-91; 9/94-97; 21/60-61)

The Luahiwa Petroglyphs are carved on 20 boulders, some of which are arranged in a semicircle and are spread over a sloping area of three acres. It is believed that a rain heiau, used for calling forth showers to aid the areas agriculture, is also on this hillside.

APPENDIX A:
SELECTED SITES FOR VISITORS

Most visitors to Maui will be staying either in the Lahaina/Kāʻana-pali region of West Maui or in the Kīhei/Wailea area of South Maui. If one is in the former region, sites 1 and 2 are easily accessible and sites 6 through 10. In the latter area, sites 19 and 21 are the most easily seen. Wherever one is staying on Maui, ʻĪao Valley (site 12) is a must and can be visited on the way to or from Kahului airport. Also in this area is the Bailey House Museum, (808) 244-3326, at 2375-A Main Street in Wailuku. It would also be important to visit Haleakalā (site 24), which would require a minimum half-day excursion. Many visitors will drive out to Hāna in a day, stopping at the Keʻanae (site 33) overlook, viewing Hāna Bay (Kaʻuiki Head, site 30), and quickly taking in Kīpahulu with a stop at the ʻOheʻo pools (site 27) and the National Park information center. But that is definitely a rushed agenda. It is highly recommended to spend at least a night (if not more) in Hāna in order to absorb the East Maui sites more slowly. The small Hāna Cultural Center and Museum, (808) 248-8622, on Uakea Road near Hāna Bay is also worth a stop.

The historic Lahaina fortress ruins can be seen at site 6 on Maui.

Ancient Hawaiian artifacts can be seen at the Bailey House Museum in Wailuku. A petroglyph fragment from Olowalu and implements used in food preparation are on display.

On Moloka'i, a view of Hālawa Valley (site 1) and bay from the overlook and down on the beach is well worth the drive to the eastern end of the island, even if one does not hike into the valley. The South Shore Fishponds (Site 5) are easily viewed during the drive to and from Hālawa. The Kapuāiwa Coconut Grove (site 8) is viewed from the highway just west of Kaunakakai. It is also worth the drive up to Pālā'au State Park to see the phallic rock, Kauleonānāhoa (site 12), and at the very least to see Kalaupapa peninsula (site 13) from the scenic overlook. On the way, stop at the Moloka'i Museum and Cultural Center, (808) 567-6436, Route 470, in Kala'e.

Visiting ancient sites on Lāna'i requires driving on unpaved roads. However, guided tours to all the sites can be arranged through the resort hotels. Sites 5 through 7, Pu'u Pehe (Sweetheart Rock), Hulopo'e, and Kapiha'a Village Interpretive Trail are easily seen if one is staying at or can get to the Four Seasons Resort or Hulopo'e Beach Park. The Lāna'i Culture and Heritage Center, (808) 565-7177, right in Lāna'i City at 730 Lāna'i Avenue, Suite 118, is worth a stop.

Driving along the south shore of Moloka'i provides many opportunities to witness the wonder of the South Shore Fishponds (site 5).

Fronting the Four Seasons Resort at Manele Bay are the village ruins of old Hulopoʻe. At the Lānaʻi Culture and Heritage Center in town are numerous informational displays and collections of ancient artifacts, including this petroglyph fragment.

APPENDIX B:
COLLECTIONS
AND CULTURAL EVENTS

ocal museums have collected many artifacts and assembled a good deal of information concerning the ancient sites of the Hawaiian Islands. The Bishop Museum, located in Honolulu, has the most extensive collection of Pacific Island material in the world. In addition to its artifacts, this museum has an exemplary research library, and its scientific and cultural departments sponsor numerous research projects, lectures, classes, and educational activities.

Bishop Museum
1525 Bernice Street
Honolulu, Oʻahu, Hawaiʻi
(808) 848-4129 or 847-3511
Hours: Daily, 9 AM to 5 PM
Admission fee

On Maui, the best collections of ancient Hawaiian and early historic artifacts and information can be found at the Maui Historical Society's Bailey House Museum in Wailuku and at the Hāna Cultural Center and Museum in Hāna.

Bailey House Museum
2375-A Main Street
Wailuku, Maui, Hawaiʻi 96793
(808) 244-3326
Hours: Monday through Friday, 10 AM to 4 PM

Hāna Cultural Center and Museum
Uakea Road near Hāna Bay
Hāna, Maui, Hawaiʻi
Phone: (808) 248-8622.
Hours: Monday through Saturday, 11 AM to 4 PM

Some hotels, particularly in Kīhei and Kāʻanapali, have small collections of artifacts that were excavated at the time of their construction. Other hotels and resorts display modern replicas of ancient artifacts. The Ritz-Carlton at Kapalua has an annual Easter weekend festival, "Celebration of the Arts," which focuses on current Hawaiian cultural issues and artistic pursuits (www.celebrationofthearts.org.).

On the grounds of Piʻilanihale Heiau (site 32) in Hana a collection of grinding stones can be found.

Molokaʻi Museum and Cultural Center is focused around the restored 1878 R.W. Meyer Sugar Mill of historic times. However, a small display of early Hawaiian artifacts can be found at the museum, and occasional lectures and cultural presentations on ancient Molokaʻi are offered from time to time.

Molokaʻi Museum and Cultural Center
Route 470
Kalaʻe, Molokaʻi, Hawaiʻi
Phone: (808) 567-6436
Email: mmcc@aloha.net
Hours: Monday through Saturday, 10 AM to 2 PM

Molokaʻi is known for its dog petroglyphs. This one is from Kawela Battleground (site 6).

The Lāna'i Culture and Heritage Center is a small museum and community cultural center, well worth a visit.

Lāna'i Culture and Heritage Center
730 Lāna'i Avenue, Suite 118
Lāna'i City, HI 96763
Phone: (808) 565-7177
www.lanaichc.org

A curious historic petroglyph from an 1876-1878 boundary commission survey can be seen on the Kaunolū Gulch cliff face marking the station point and boundary between Kaunolū and Keālia Kapu ahupua'a.

APPENDIX C:
PRESERVATION

The ancient sites of Maui, Moloka'i and Lāna'i are cultural treasures and, as such, are invaluable to all people, of all ethnic backgrounds, for all time. They provide spiritual inspiration, as well as irreplaceable knowledge. The archaeological resources of all the Hawaiian Islands need to be protected against natural destructive forces, as well as careless individuals and groups seeking short-term gain.

Since the Antiquities Act of 1906, numerous federal laws have been passed by the United States Congress to help protect and conserve the ancient sites located on public lands and reservations throughout America. The National Historic Preservation Act of 1966 is a particularly effective piece of legislation in this regard. As a result of such legislation, many sites have been listed on the national and state registers in order to secure official recognition of their significance as historic places and to aid in their preservation. Oddly enough, actual protection is not guaranteed for these sites unless they fall within special county-zoned districts or state conservation areas.

Neither federal laws, nor similar state laws, can protect all sites, especially those on private property, where landowners may knowingly or unknowingly destroy important contextual evidence as well as valuable artifacts. Hawai'i State law requires site surveys of both public and private lands slated for development, but, because the developer hires the archaeologist, a conflict of interest may arise, even if only in theory. Therefore, even with the survey reviews provided by the State Historic Preservation Division of the Department of Land and Natural Resources, weak links in the preservation process can occur.

Public interest and understanding are necessary for any law to be truly effective. Each citizen has a role to play and must take at least partial responsibility for the preservation of ancient sites. Only through vocal support and local action can historic and prehistoric sites be protected from natural deterioration, vandalism, and the rapid, sometimes thoughtless, land development of the kind that has already devastated an estimated two-thirds of the known ancient sites on O'ahu.

To combat further destruction of ancient Hawaiian sites, tour the accessible sites and educate yourself and others about them so that you and your family gain an understanding of the importance of such places. When you see preliminary signs of land-use change or development, ask the landowner (or the state) if the site has been surveyed by an archaeologist. And, as the National Park Service recommends, when you visit an ancient site, take nothing but photographs and leave nothing but footprints.

Some organizations promoting the preservation and appreciation of ancient sites in Hawai'i are:

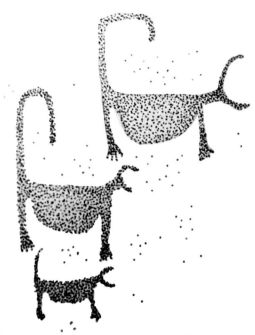

Moloka'i dog petroglyphs from the Kawela Battleground (site 6), on Moloka'i.

Historic Hawai'i Foundation
680 Iwilei Road, Suite 690
Honolulu, HI 96817
www.historichawaii.org

State Historic Preservation
Department of Land and Natural Resources
601 Kamokila Blvd., Rm. 555
Kapolei, HI 96707
www.dlnr.hawaii.gov/shpd

National Park Service
300 Ala Moana Blvd.
Rm. 6-226
Honolulu, HI 96850
www.nps.gov

Society for Hawaiian Archaeology
P.O. Box 23292
Honolulu, HI 96823
www.hawaiianarchaeology.org

APPENDIX D:
HAWAIIAN PRONUNCIATION

Hawaiian is a lovely, melodious language. The alphabet, developed by missionaries from the oral language of ancient Hawai'i, comprises thirteen letters: These are seven consonants, h, k, l, m, n, p, w, as well as the 'okina (see below), and five vowels, a, e, i, o, u.

Pronunciation of the consonants is roughly similar to that of their English counterparts. The letter w is the most different, usually pronounced like a v after i and e, and like a w after u and o. When w is the first letter, it can be pronounced either v or w.

All words end in a vowel and vowels are generously used, sometimes in surprising combinations by comparison to English usage. Many words consist solely of vowel clusters. Thus, the following sentence becomes possible in Hawaiian: I 'Aiea I 'ai 'ia ai ia I'a. (In [the town of] 'Aiea the aforementioned fish was eaten.)

Hawaiian vowels are generally pronounced as their equivalents in Spanish and Japanese. However, with the addition of a glottal stop, called 'okina (written as an inverted apostrophe in front of a vowel: 'a), or a macron, called a kahakō (written as a horizontal line over a vowel: ā), the sound quality of the vowel changes. Many Hawaiian language specialists consider the 'okina to be the eighth consonant.

The glottal stop is common in many Polynesian languages. It can be described as a momentary stoppage of the airflow passing through the glottis, producing a sudden small thrust of air not unlike a tiny cough. The closest equivalent in English might be the catch of air in the utterance of "Oh-oh!" when something is amiss.

The macron doubles the sound length of a vowel.

The proper use of the glottal stop and the macron is critical to correct pronunciation of Hawaiian words. Many words whose letter spelling is the same have very different meanings depending on the presence or absence of these two marks:

kau = to place, put, hang
kāu = your, yours
ka'u = my, mine
Ka'ū = name of a district on the island of Hawai'i

Diacritical markings in the text have been used in accordance with contemporary usage as predicated on recommendations of *ʻAhahui ʻŌlelo Hawaiʻi* (1978) and the Pukui-Elbert *Hawaiian Dictionary* (1986). However, the numerous references and quotes in this book taken from *ʻŌlelo Noʻeau, Hawaiian Proverbs & Poetical Sayings*, by Mary Kawena Pukui, retain the original orthography that reflects an older practice.

This drawing of a double birdman petroglyph that is found together with other carved and abraded images of birds, dogs, and human figures at Pōʻāiwa Petroglyphs (site 2) on Lānaʻi.

Determining the proper use of diacritical markings in place names can be particularly challenging. A standard reference work on this subject is *Place Names of Hawaiʻi* (1981). Unfortunately, many locations are not listed in that book. Important areas are well known and easily recognizable; other remote locations, however, have been lost to lava, to bulldozers, or to our memory. In the absence of an unbroken oral tradition (Hawaiian was actively suppressed following the overthrow of the monarchy in 1893), the pronunciation as well as the meaning of many words has also vanished or been distorted. This book follows current practice in the use of diacritical markings: People's names and place names whose pronunciation cannot be verified have been left unmarked.

—David L. Eyre

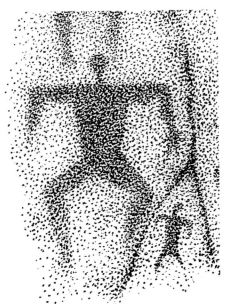

Petroglyph of human figures at Nuʻu Landing on Maui.

GLOSSARY OF TERMS

ʻaʻā	Rough, clinker lava.
ahu	Heap of stones.
ahupuaʻa	Land division.
akua	God, goddess, image, idol, spirit.
akua kiʻi	Image representing a god.
ala	Path, way, or trail.
ʻalā	Smooth, water-worn lava stones.
aliʻi	Chief, chiefess, king, queen, royalty, nobility.
aloha	Hello, goodbye, warm greeting, love.
ʻamaʻama	Young mullet fish.
ʻanae	Full-sized ʻamaʻama mullet fish.
ʻanuʻu	Ancient heiau tower.
ʻaumakua	Ancestral spirit or personal god. (Pl.) ʻaumākua.
awa	Milkfish.
ʻawa	Plant root used to make a narcotic drink.
Haʻikū	Region of Maui Island.
haku mele	Poet, one who composes a chant.
hālau	School, place of training.
hale	House, building, home place.
hale mana	Large house in a luakini temple.
hale noa	House where entire family could meet without kapu.
Haleakalā	"House of the sun." Mountain crater and national park.
Hale o Lono	Temples dedicated to Lono, god of agriculture.
hale pahu	Drum house.
Hāna	District of East Maui.
hauola	"Dew of life."
Hawaiʻi	The island group as a state; also, the largest and most recently formed island of the group, also called the Big Island.

heiau	Hawaiian temple, place of worship or offering; stone platform or earth terrace.
heiau ho'o ulu'ai	Temple devoted to increase of food supply.
heiau ho'o ulu i'a	Temple to promote the increase of fishing.
heiau ho'oulu ua	Temple to insure rainfall.
heiau ma'o	Temple to promote food.
Hina	Hawaiian moon goddess and mother of demi-god Māui.
holehole	To peel, to strip off.
hōlua	Ancient Hawaiian sport, sled course, slide.
Honolulu	"Sheltered bay." Capital city of the State of Hawai'i on the island of O'ahu.
ho'okupu	Gifts, sprout.
ho'omalu	to protect, to shelter.
hula	Ancient and modern art of dance.
'Īao	"Dawning inspiration." Fish, bird, the planet Jupiter, valley and state park.
'ie'ie	Vine growing in high country.
'ili'ili	Pebble, small rock. Used as hula stones.
Kā'anapali	District of West Maui.
ka'ao	Fanciful tale.
kaha ki'i	Scratched or drawn images.
kahakō	Macron.
Kahekili	16th century Maui high chief.
Kahiki	Anyplace "abroad." legendary island home of the ancient Hawaiians; thought by some to be Tahiti.
kāhili	Royal feather standard.
Kaho'olawe	Name of one of the Hawaiian Islands.
kahu	Guardian, priest, keeper.
kahuna	Priest, shaman, expert, master. (Pl.) kāhuna.
kahuna hana 'upena	Master fishnet maker.
kahuna ho'okele	Navigator.
kahuna ho'oulu 'ai	Agricultural expert.
kahuna kālai	Carving expert, sculptor.
kahuna kuhikuhipu'uone	Architect.
kahuna lapa'au	Medical practitioner, healer.
kahuna nui	High priest.
kai	Sea water, salt water.

Keka'a	Hill of "thunder." Black Rock at Kā'anapali in West Maui.
kalo	Taro.
kama'āina	Child of the land, native-born, familiar; now commonly used to mean long-time resident.
Kamapua'a	Name of pig god.
Kamehameha	Name of a line of Hawai'i Island chiefs/monarchs.
kanaka maoli	Full-blooded Hawaiian.
Kanaloa	God of the oceans.
kāne	Man, male, husband (Cap.) God of freshwater sources.
kapa	Tapa, barkcloth.
kapu	Taboo, forbidden, sacred, consecrated.
kauā	Outcast person.
Kaua'i	Name of one of the Hawaiian Islands.
kāula	Seer, prophet.
Kaupō	Region of East Maui.
kī	Ti, a woody plant of the lily family whose leaves are often used in rituals, as well as in everyday life.
ki'i	Image, statue, picture.
ki'i pōhaku	Petroglyphs, images carved in stone.
Kīpahulu	Region of East Maui.
koa	Largest of the native forest trees; warrior; brave.
ko'a	Fishing shrine; coral; coral head; fishing grounds.
ko'i	Adze hammer.
Kona	Leeward sides of the Hawaiian Islands.
kōnane	Ancient game resembling checkers.
konohiki	Overseer of land and fishing rights.
Ko'olau	Windward sides of the Hawaiian Islands.
kū	To stand; stop (Cap.) God of war.
kua 'aina	Backside or back-country.
kuapā	Fishpond walls.
kuhina nui	Prime minister.
kūkae	Excrement.
Kula	Region of upcountry Maui.
kupua	Spirit being that can change its shape from one form into another. Demigod or hero.
kū'ula	Altar or stone used to worship or attract fish or fishgods.

Lahaina	District and town in West Maui.
Lānaʻi	Name of one of the Hawaiian Islands.
lapaʻau	Medical practice; to heal, cure.
lei	Flower garland.
leina a ka ʻuhane	"Leaping place of the spirits."
lele	An altar, offering stand.
lele kawa	Cliff jumping.
limu	General name for underwater plants; seaweed.
loʻi	Taro paddy.
loko	Pond or fishpond.
loko iʻa kalo	Shallow fishpond and taro paddy.
loko kuapā	Walled fishpond.
loko puʻuone	Fishpond separated from the ocean by a sand dune and fed by streams, springs, or both.
loko ʻume iki	Large walled fishtrap.
Lono	God of agriculture, peace, and Makahiki.
lua	Pit, indentation, hole.
luakini heiau	Hawaiian temple where ruling chiefs prayed and human sacrifices were offered.
luapaʻū	Refuse pit found at luakini heiau.
maile	Native twining vine.
mahalo	Thank you.
mākāhā	Sluice gates used in fishponds.
malihini	Newcomer, of foreign origin.
Makahiki	(Cap.) Ancient festival beginning about mid-October and lasting four months. Sport and religious festivities were conducted at this time and war was kapu.
makai	Towards the ocean.
Makawao	District of Maui Island.
mana	Spiritual, divine, or miraculous power.
Mānaiakalani	Ceremonial hook used to pierce the mouth of a human sacrifice.
manini	Common reef surgeonfish.
Maui	Name of one of the Hawaiian Islands.
Māui	Name of a demigod.
mauka	Towards the mountains.
menehune	Legendary race of small people who worked at night during prehistoric times building temples, roads, fishponds, and other structures.

moa pahe'e	Dart sliding game.
mō'ī	High chief, king.
Mokuhinia	Royal fishpond in Lahaina, Maui.
Moku'ula	Sacred island in ancient Lahaina.
moku	Large land district.
Moloka'i	Name of one of the Hawaiian Islands.
mo'o	Lizard, reptile, dragon, serpent.
mo'olelo	Myth, tradition, history, story.
O'ahu	Name of one of the Hawaiian Islands.
'ōhi'a	Two kinds of trees, the mountain apple and the lehua blossom bearer.
'okina	Glottal stop.
Olowalu	"Many hills." Region in Lahaina district of Maui.
'ō'ō	Endemic bird to Hawai'i, now extinct.
'ō'ō ihe	Spear throwing.
'o'opu	Goby, a fish.
'ōpae'oeha'a	Clawed shrimp.
ōpū	Temple tower.
Pā'ao	Traditional tenth-to-thirteenth-century kahuna believed to have brought a colony to Hawai'i from the South Pacific, possibly Tahiti. Said to have introduced human sacrifice.
pāhoehoe	Smooth or ropy lava.
pahu	Drum.
pali	Cliff, precipice.
pānānā	"Sighting wall."
paniolo	Cowboy.
Papa	Primal mother goddess.
pāpio	Young jackfish.
pele	Volcano, lava (Cap.) Volcano goddess.
Pi'ilani	16th century Maui high chief.
piko	Umbilical cord stump, navel.
pili	A grass used for thatching.
pipi	Cattle.
Pō	The realm of the gods; night; darkness.
pōhaku	Rock, stone.
Pōhaku o Kāne	Sacred stone.
pono	Righteous, upright, moral.
pua'a	Pig or boar.

puhi	Moray eel.
puka	Hole or opening; also, to proclaim or speak.
puʻu	Any kind of protuberance, bulge, heap, pile, mound, hill, peak.
puʻuhonua	Place of refuge, sanctuary.
tapa	(See kapa.)
taro	(See kalo.)
ti	(See kī.)
tsunami	Tidal wave (Japanese).
ulua	Jackfish.
ʻulu maika	A disk-rolling game.
ʻumeke	Calabash.
waʻa	Dugout canoe.
wahi pana	Sacred or legendary place.
wai	Fresh water; any liquid other than sea water.
wai ea	A small thatched house within the temple precinct where incantations were invoked.
waiwai	Richness.
Wākea	Primal father god.

These two boxers engaged in mokomoko
appear on a cliff face in Kalaʻilinui Gulch
in Makawao on Maui.

SELECTED BIBLIOGRAPHY

1. Beckwith, M. 1976. *Hawaiian Mythology.* Honolulu: University of Hawai'i Press.

2. Belknap, J.P. 1981. *Kaanapali.* Honolulu: Amfac Property Corporation.

3. Chapman, P. and P.V. Kirch. 1979. *Archaeological Excavations at Seven Sites Southeast Maui.* Honolulu: Bishop Museum Press (Report 79-1)

4. Clark, J. 1989. *The Beaches of Maui County.* Honolulu: University of Hawai'i Press.

5. Cordy, R. 1987. *Piilanihale Heiau Project: Phase 1. Site Report.* Honolulu: Bishop Museum Press (Report 70-9).

6. Cox, J. H. and E. Stasack. 1970. *Hawaiian Petroglyphs.* Honolulu: Bishop Museum Press.

7. Dale, P.W. 1969. *Seventy North to Fifty South: Captain Cook's Last Voyage.* Englewood, N.J.: Prentice-Hall.

8. Emory, K.P. 1921. *An Archaeological Survey of Haleakala.* Occasional Papers 7(11): 235-259 (1-25). Honolulu: Bishop Museum.

9._____1986. *The Island of Lāna'i: A Survey of Native Culture.* Honolulu: Bishop Museum Press.

10._____and R. Hommon. 1972. *Endangered Hawaiian Archaeological Sites within Maui County.* Honolulu: Bishop Museum 72-2.

11. Estioko-Griffin, A. and M. Yent. 1986. *Management and Interpretive Plans for Halekii-Pihana Heiau State Monument.* State of Hawai'i, Department of Land & Natural Resources, State Parks.

12. Gay, L.K. 1983. *True Stories of the Island of Lāna'i.* Honolulu: Rogers Printing Inc.

13. James, V. 1998. *Ancient Sites of O'ahu: Archaeological Places of Interest in the Hawaiian Islands.* Honolulu: Bishop Museum Press.

14. Kalakaua, D. 1990. *The Legends and Myths of Hawai'i.* Honolulu: Mutual Publishing.

15. Kamakau, S. 1961. *Ruling Chiefs of Hawai'i* (Haleki'i p. 82-87) Honolulu: Bishop Museum Press.

16._____ 1976. *The Works of the People of Old.* Honolulu: Bishop Museum Press.

17. Kepler, A. 1987. *Maui's Hana Highway.* Honolulu: Mutual Publishing.

18._____ 1992. *Sunny South Maui: A Guide to Kihei, Wailea and Makena.* Honolulu: Mutual Publishing.

19. Kepler, A. and C. Kepler. 1991. *Majestic Molokai: A Nature Lover's Guide.* Honolulu: Mutual Publishing.

20. Kirch, P.V. 1985. Feathered Gods and Fishhooks. Honolulu: University of Hawai'i Press.

21. _____ 1996. *Legacy of the Landscape: An Illustrated Guide to Hawaiian Archaeological Sites.* Honolulu: University of Hawai'i Press.

22. _____ 2012. *A Shark Going Inland is My Chief: The Island Civilization of Ancient Hawai'i.* Berkeley: University of California Press.

23. _____ 2014. *Kua'āina Kahiko: Life and Land in Ancient Kahikinui, Maui.* Honolulu: University of Hawai'I Press.

24. Kwiatkowski, P.F. 1991. *Na Ki'i Pōhaku: A Hawaiian Petroglyph Primer.* Honolulu: Ku Pa'a Inc.

25. Lee, P. and K. Willis. 1987. *Tales of the Night Rainbow.* Honolulu: Paia-Kapela-Willis 'Ohana, Inc.

26. Maly, K. and O. Maly. 2011. *Hanohano Lāna'i—Lāna'i is Distinguished: An Ethnography of Ka'ā Ahupua'a and the Island of Lāna'i.* Kaneohe, Hawai'i: Kumu Pono Associates LLC.

27. Maunupau, T.K. 1998. Huakai Makaikai a Kaupo, Maui: A Visit to Kaupō, Maui. Honolulu: Bishop Museum Press.

28. McBride, L.R. 1969. *Petroglyphs of Hawai'i.* Hilo: Petroglyph Press.

29. Ne, H. with G. L. Cronin. 1992. *Tales of Molokai: The Voice of Harriet Ne.* Honolulu: University of Hawai'i Press.

30. Pearson, R. and R. Hommon. 1970. *The Archaeology of Hana: Preliminary Survey of Waianapanapa State Park.* Honolulu: Hawai'i State Archaeological Journal 70-2.

31. Pukui, M.K. and S. Elbert. 1983. *'Ōlelo No'eau: Hawaiian Proverbs and Poetical Sayings.* Honolulu: University of Hawai'i Press.

32. _____and E. Mookini. 1976. *Place Names of Hawai'i.* Honolulu: University of Hawai'i Press.

33. Pukui, M.K. and C. Curtis. 1974. *The Water of Kane and Other Legends of the Hawaiian Islands.* Honolulu: Kamehameha Schools Press.

34. _____ 1971. *Tales of the Menehune and Other Legends of the Hawaiian Islands.* Honolulu: Kamehameha Schools Press.

35. Silva, C. 1986. *Historical Report: Haleki'i-Pihana State Monument.* State of Hawai'i, Department of Land and Natural Resources, State Parks.

36. Soehren, L. 1963. *An Archaeological Survey of Portions of East Maui.* Honolulu: Bishop Museum.

37. Sterling, E.P. 1998. *Sites of Maui.* Honolulu: Bishop Museum Press.

38. Summers, C.C. 1990. *Molokai: A Site Survey.* Number 14, Pacific Anthropological Record. Honolulu: Bishop Museum.

39. Valeri, V. 1985. *Kingship and Sacrifice.* Chicago: University of Chicago Press.

40. Walker, W.M. 1931. *Archaeology of Maui (Manuscript).* Honolulu: Bishop Museum.

41. Wyban, C.A. 1992. *Tide and Current: Fishponds of Hawai'i.* Honolulu: University of Hawai'i Press.

42. Yent, M. 1993. *Archaeological Restoration Plan: Portion of Pihana Heiau Hale-kii-Pihana Heiaus State Monument, Paukukalo, Wailuku, Maui.* (TMK: 3-4-30:4). State of Hawai'i, Dept. of Land & Natural Resources, State Parks.

43. Youngblood, R. 1983. *On the Hana Coast.* Honolulu: Emphasis International Ltd./Link Inc.

On a South Maui rock outcropping, two abraded petroglyph figures echo each other's waving gesture. Muscular, triangular body types like the one on the left may have been introduced around 1300. Note the triangular, horned heads of the two figures.